Foreword

The residents of certain local authority housing estates suffer relatively high levels of victimisation from crime. In addition, their residential environments may be vandalised and poorly maintained. A variety of initiatives going back to the 1970s have been employed to improve conditions on such estates, partly in the hope that the quality of community life will be improved and that crime levels may be reduced. Prominent amongst these is the Priority Estates Project (PEP), sponsored by the Department of the Environment. The research reported here forms part of a joint project with the Department of the Environment to assess the impact of the Priority Estates Project on housing service delivery, crime and community life. This report focuses on the effect which PEP may have on levels of crime and on community relations.

The findings contained in this study are both rich and complex. Certainly, there is support for the positive effect on crime expected of PEP but there is also worrying evidence of how crime can grow on hard-pressed estates, particularly those which house substantial numbers of poor residents. In general, the report provides evidence of PEP's impact on crime but also points to the need to complement such programmes with other efforts to tackle the growth of crime on 'problem' housing estates.

ROGER TARLING

Head of the Research and Planning Unit

Acknowledgements

I would like to thank Professor Paul Rock who supervised my part of the research, Lizanne Dowds, Tim Hope and Paul Ekblom of the Home Office who managed the project, Keith Bottomley at the University of Hull for his assistance and Moira Parkes for transcribing the interview data. Although I would like to name all of the people who contributed to the research individually, I will thank them corporately: the staff of Hull City Council and the London Borough of Tower Hamlets, the Metropolitan Police and Humberside Constabulary, staff and students at the local school in Hull which, in order to protect the identity of the estate, cannot be named, and the PEP consultants and tenant support workers. Finally, I am indebted to all the tenants on both the PEP estates who gave me their time, endless cups of tea and often fed me while telling me about their estates.

J.F

In addition to those corporate bodies mentioned above I should like to thank the following individuals—in no particular order—for their help and advice at various stages and in various ways during the course of a long project: Lizanne Dowds, Mike Sutton, Paul Rock, Howard Glennerster, Tessa Turner, Patrick Allen, Paul Wiles, Anne Power, Tricia Zipfel, Ginny Shaw, David Riley, Philip Mercieca (for his work both at the Harris Research Centre and at Research Surveys of Great Britain Ltd.), Norman Davidson, Frank Palin, Chris Hale, Paul Ekblom, Mike Burbidge, Wesley Skogan, Derek Cornish, John MacLeod, Roy Walmsley and, last but not least, my co-author. Above all, though, my thanks are due to Mary Tuck, former Head of the Research and Planning Unit, without whose support, encouragement and persuasiveness this study would probably not have started.

T.H.

Contents

Summary

This study reports the main findings of research supported by the Home Office Research and Planning Unit into the impact of the Priority Estates Project (PEP) on crime and community life.

Background

The Priority Estates Project, sponsored by the Department of the Environment, works with the local authorities and tenants of some of Britain's most difficult and run-down estates to institute changes in the delivery of local housing services and management and to involve tenants in the day-to-day running of their estates. Since PEP promises to bring about improvements to estates which are also likely to have high crime levels it was felt important to investigate its potential for reducing crime in more detail.

Though crime prevention is not a specific task of the PEP model, the research was designed to ascertain whether PEP might reduce crime. Four means of prevention are represented in PEP's approach:

i. creating better dwelling security and more 'defensible space';

ii. halting the spiral of deterioration, tackling vandalism, caretaking, cleaning up the estate, thereby reducing the 'signs of disorder' and fear of crime, and signifying that the estate is well-cared-for;

iii. investing in the estate so that residents will develop a positive view and thus a greater stake in their community, and a greater expectation of law-abiding behaviour;

iv. increasing informal community control over crime both through increased surveillance and supervision by residents and housing officials and facilitating the development of a set of norms and expectations against offending on the estate.

These ideas were used to guide the conduct and analysis of the research.

The Research Project

The research project, commissioned by the Home Office and the Department of the Environment, started in 1987. The progress of two new PEPs was studied over a period of three years. One PEP estate was located in the London Borough of Tower Hamlets, the other in the City of Kingston-upon-Hull. The London PEP consisted of two relatively small adjacent estates (about 440 dwellings in all). The Hull PEP estate was larger (about 1,100 dwellings), forming part of an even bigger council housing development on the outskirts of the city. Two 'control' estates were selected for comparison, one in Tower Hamlets and one in Hull. An effort was made to select estates which were broadly similar in architectural design and social composition.

Progress on the PEP estates in comparison with their control estates was studied in a variety of ways including 'before' and 'after' household surveys on the PEP and control estates, and detailed ethnographic observation and interviews with tenants over periods of 18 months on the London PEP estate and 12 months in Hull. A parallel study of changes in housing services, management and environmental conditions was funded by the Department of the Environment and will be published as a separate report authored by Howard Glennerster and Tessa Turner.

Findings

Community and crime on the estates

At the outset of the study the two estates selected to become new PEPs both had high crime rates and adverse design and social characteristics. However, the Hull estate conformed more closely to the typical image of the problem estate on which PEP works—it was larger, poorer and seemed more disorganised. Importantly, although the estates had comparable levels of more serious offences—burglary and motor crime in particular—the Hull estate had a greater level of disorderliness, associated with youth in particular, which fostered a greater sense of insecurity amongst residents, particularly women. Nevertheless, despite the difficulties of both estates, a certain basic and low-level degree of neighbourliness seemed to survive—a potential which PEP might be able to develop.

Implementing PEP: the tenant's perspective

The basic elements of PEP's housing service model—a local estate office, repairs, caretaking, lettings—were implemented on both estates. However, in the first year of operation on the London experimental estate, the local estate office was run by a housing manager who appeared to have little sympathy with the PEP approach, causing friction with the tenants and the PEP consultant. While some estates services improved, the staff problems led to disputes and the temporary withdrawal of PEP. Tenant enthusiasm and co-operation never properly recovered from the earlier disappointments, despite the hard work by other housing staff and PEP workers.

In contrast, the issue of tenant management dominated PEP's work on the Hull estate leading to the formation of the Neighbourhood Management Committee (NMC) with directly elected tenant representatives. About £1.5m was allocated by Estates Action for planned maintenance to improve the weather resistance of the system-built houses. In addition, some £1.3m was allocated for environment improvements, following tenant consultation, to increase the amount of 'defensible space' on the estate. At the end of the study period these latter improvements had only been completed for about half the area of houses.

Community change on the London PEP estate

At the end of the study period, residents' feelings about the London estate were mixed, reflecting the varied experiences of the past three years. PEP did bring a greater sense of security and a real increase in the Bengali residents' feelings of safety from racially-motivated victimisation. Nevertheless, despite the better prospects for the Bengali residents, the other residents on the London experimental estate had become poorer, more socially heterogenous, and more apathetic.

Community change on the Hull PEP estate

The ethnographic research found the estate community to be socially fragmented. The established tenants had managed to insulate themselves, by and large, from the remainder who were generally more vulnerable to adverse economic and personal experiences and misfortunes. Amongst the vulnerable tenants could be found a number of crime-prone groups: networks of adults stealing and receiving stolen goods, and unruly teenagers who caused trouble to an extent far beyond their numbers.

Changes in environmental design, tenant consultation and population characteristics—the last as a result of tenant allocations—occurred during the study period, interacting with each other and with the pre-existing estate culture. The physical changes helped create different levels of vacancies in different parts of the estate and, given the worsening financial circumstances of the newcomers, the populations in the different parts of the estate diverged. Both the design improvements, and the general sense of optimism generated by PEP, provided support for the more stable and established tenants who began to exude a greater confidence about the estate and the possibility of improvement. Yet, at the same time, a greater number of young poor people and those discharged from institutional care were coming onto the estate. Their arrival at a time of high unemployment and into conditions of poverty created a destabilising influence, swelled the numbers of vulnerable tenants, and encouraged more disorderly activities and lifestyles.

The London experience: stability

Although crime rates declined on the London PEP estate, they fell by a greater extent on the London control estate. The scale of the reductions, especially on the control estate, illustrates the volatility of crime rates in small residential areas. Quite sharp changes in crime and disorder on the experimental estate, occurring at times when the local office was inactive, also illustrate the highly localised nature of crime on the estates. The greater decline in crime on the control estate than the experimental estate may have been due to a combination of good locally-based housing managers—themselves implementing many of the ingredients of the PEP model—increased physical security, and greater residential surveillance, stemming in part at least from the stabilising influence of a substantial Bengali community on the estate.

Although intra-neighbour tensions remained on the London experimental estate, which saw a relatively greater increase in residents' worries about person-related disorder, the estate did not have a threatening youthful presence. As such, the failure to energise all sections of the estate community may not have had particularly harmful consequences.

The Hull experience: conflicting forces

On the Hull experimental estate, environmental design modifications and improvements in management quality and tenant involvement interacted with changes in tenant turnover and allocation to the estate. Their combined effect was to alter the internal 'culture' of the estate to produce an intensification *both* of social control and criminality which found expression in differences between parts of the estate and various groups of tenants. Though much had been achieved on the experimental estate in Hull, nothing had managed to halt the turnover of tenants to the estate as a whole.

A plausible interpretation of the events on the Hull experimental estate is that the environmental improvements did reduce the number of vacancies in one part of the estate because the new 'defensible space' environment was valued by its residents. Therefore, of the incoming residents—who were relatively poorer and less likely to be in two-parent family units—those with children were allocated available houses and those without were placed in flats in the tower blocks on the estate. Territoriality, social cohesion and 'empowerment' increased amongst the residents of the houses as a result of environmental modifications and PEP's efforts to involve them in the improvement of services and estate management. However, the newly-arrived single-parent families who were housed there stood out as especially vulnerable to crime.

Despite a programme of improvements to the security of the tower blocks, and better management of the estate as a whole, the newcomers—that is, the young, childless poor—displaced many of the previous, elderly residents and attracted crime to themselves, both as perpetrators and victims, concentrating crime in their part of the estate.

Conclusions

A number of examples of crime reduction were found to have occurred on the experimental estates—in contrast to their comparable 'control' estates—which both the ethnographic research and the analysis of survey data suggest did indeed bring about reductions in crime and disorder.

Together, these examples suggest that the PEP model does have a real potential for reducing crime.

However, on the estates studied during this research, all of the successes were only partial—they occurred in either one or the other of the experimental estates, or only for particular areas or groups of residents in each estate. Two obstacles to the wider effectiveness of the PEP model on the estates studied were: first, the 'quality' of implementation; and second, the instability of residential communities arising from population turnover, social heterogeneity and the 'subterranean culture' within estate communities.

The lesson for crime prevention from the experience of the London experimental estate is that multi-agency collaboration and community organisation—at least at the very local level—may depend as much if not more upon the quality of professionals involved than upon the organisational structures which are put in place.

On the Hull experimental estate, not only were many of the tenants keen to become involved in the estate but actually began to attain some degree of empowerment through a resident-elected Neighbourhood Management Committee (NMC). Yet there was a worrying increase in crime and disorder, at least in one part of the estate, which was only just being contained at the close of the research.

The capacity of the PEP model to bring about community organisation and involvement may be affected by the rate of population turnover and degree of social and cultural heterogeneity within the community. Of all the estates studied, the London control estate achieved the greatest social stability, mainly because the Bengali community ceased to be a minority group and came to comprise a major presence on the estate. On the London experimental estate, PEP was able to empower the Bengalis as a group so that they too were able to achieve a 'presence' on the estate. It was particularly their participation in the tenants association which resulted in the use of appropriate structures and procedures to deal with the problems which faced them. The white residents were a more disparate and heterogeneous group, reacting with apathy but feeling resentful of the empowerment of the Bengali community.

On the Hull experimental estate, the implementation of the PEP model did seem to lead to some degree of social stability—particularly amongst the longer-term residents of the houses which had or were about to receive environmental improvements—but was not extended to the community as whole. The experience vividly illustrates the interplay of 'conflicting forces'—those leading towards social stability and informal social control, which PEP helped promote; and those leading towards social disorder and a broadening of a 'subterranean culture', which the allocation of new tenants helped exacerbate.

One conclusion reached by this report is that it may not be easy to intervene in the process of allocating tenants to estates in order to forestall the concentration of social problems; in large part, this is because local housing managers have to weigh a number of factors in matching the supply of dwellings on an estate to the demand from prospective council tenants.

It is shown that the implementation of the PEP model on an estate can provide a good infrastructure for building multi-agency collaboration to tackle the problems of an estate community, but that little of this occurred on the estates studied.

Finally, a case is made for the need to address specifically the causes of youth crime—and the 'subterranean culture' which sustains it—on stressed estates, in addition to the promotion of informal social control amongst residents.

1 Introduction

The Priority Estates Project (PEP) has been sponsored by the Department of the Environment (DoE) since 1979 to work on some of Britain's difficult-to-let council estates which were poorly managed, run down and often occupied by the most disadvantaged groups in society. PEP consultants focus on particular estates and over a fixed period give support and advice to local authority housing departments and tenants to bring about improvements in their estates' management, appearance and quality of life. Some funds for estate improvements may also be made available from the DoE's Estate Action programme. This report investigates whether this kind of work can also bring about reductions in crime.

The PEP model

PEP consultants seek to reverse the deterioriation of estates through measures based on the principles of estate-based housing management and tenant involvement (Power, 1987a). The PEP model for estate improvement which was studied during this research project is that set out in the DoE's 1987 *PEP Guide to Local Housing Management* (Power, 1987b). There are ten ingredients

1. A local estate based office.

2. A local repairs team.

3. Local lettings—a local list of applicants, local procedures for signing on and allocating tenants within an agreed priority scheme.

4. Local control of rent collection and arrears.

5. Residents caretaking, cleaning and open space maintenance with local supervision.

6. Resident liaison with management—in most cases this will take the form of a residents forum acting as an advisory and consultative group.

7. Small scale capital improvements and refurbishments.

8. Well-trained local staff with delegated authority.

9. The project manager as the key figure accountable for estate management.

10. A locally-controlled estate budget for management and maintenance.

It is important to emphasise that PEP does not run or manage the estates on which it works—this remains with the local authority, though with increased involvement from tenants.[1]

The PEP consultant acts on his/her designated estate '. . . as a catalyst for change, as arbiter between tenants and council, between central and local management, between politicians and officers and tenants, between the DoE and local authorities, facilitating an autonomous local management and maintenance structure at estate level' (Anne Power quoted in Glennerster and Turner).

Unlike some other estate-based initiatives, PEP has not set out to tackle problems of crime and anti-social behaviour directly—though many of the estates where it works have high crime rates. However, during the course of PEP's work, there has been some evidence of reductions in crime-levels and in vandalism, graffiti and other aspects of disorder (Burbidge, 1984; Rock, 1988; Power, 1988). Sometimes this can be attributed to measures which have specifically tackled crime, such as improved dwelling security or estate policing, but reduced crime also seems to have happened as a consequence of the general improvements which PEP has brought about.

It was decided to mount a study to evaluate the impact of PEP on crime and community life for three reasons: in the first place, PEP is representative of a variety of estate-based crime prevention and community development initiatives, with common roots, stemming back to pioneering work by NACRO in the 1970s (see Rock, 1988 for a discussion of these), few of which, however, had been subject to rigorous, controlled evaluation. In this sense, an evaluation of PEP was thought to provide, in part at least, an assessment of this tradition of intervention on problem estates. Second, as research has suggested increasingly that the kinds of estate on which PEP usually works are likely to be those where crime and social problems are concentrated, it was thought important to assess whether the positive changes which may be brought about by PEP also extended to crime reduction. Third, the various processes which it was believed PEP embodied were similar to ideas for crime prevention being advocated in a variety of criminological work and it was thought to be desirable to have an opportunity to examine them empirically. The rationale underlying these views is described in more detail in Chapter 2.

The research project

The research described in this report was commissioned by the Home Office and the Department of the Environment in 1987. Progress on two estates where PEP was starting to work was studied over a period of three years. One

---

[1]During the period since the inception of this research, PEP, in line with the Government's thinking, has come to give greater emphasis to more formal ways of involving tenants in the day-to-day management of their estates.

PEP estate was located in the London Borough of Tower Hamlets, the other in the City of Kingston-upon-Hull. The characteristics of these estates at the start of the project are described in Chapter 3. Progress on the PEP estates in comparison with their control estates was studied in the following ways:

i. 'before' and 'after' household surveys on the PEP and control estates assessing levels of victimisation, fear of crime and tenants' perceptions of estate conditions, housing services and community life;

ii. collection of crime figures recorded by the police for the PEP estates;

iii. detailed ethnographic observation and interviews with tenants over periods of 18 months on the London PEP estate and 12 months in Hull;

iv. monitoring of management changes on the PEP estates;

v. development and analysis of performance indicators on standards of housing management during the course of the PEPs in comparison with the control estates;

vi. measurement, derived from observation, of environmental standards on the estates;

vii. evaluation of changes in the housing management process through regular observation and interview with housing staff and others.

The household surveys were commissioned, designed and analysed by the Home Office Research and Planning Unit. Fieldwork and data preparation were carried out by survey research contractors. The ethnographic research was funded by the Home Office, carried out by Dr Janet Foster and supervised by Professor Paul Rock of the London School of Economics and Political Science (LSE). The study of changes in the management and delivery of housing services, and changes in the environmental condition of the estates, was funded by the Department of the Environment and undertaken by Professor Howard Glennerster and Ms Tessa Turner also of the LSE. This present report focuses principally on the impact of PEP on crime and community relations as uncovered by the surveys and ethnography, though it draws, where appropriate, on findings from the other aspects of the project.[2]

Research design

The quantitative estimation of the effects of social interventions is not straightforward and certain methodological pitfalls need to be avoided, especially in research designs such as this, which cannot rely upon random assignment of subjects to experimental and control groups (Judd and Kenny,

---

[2]Glennerster and Turner's study will be the focus of a separate report to be published by the Department of the Environment.

1981). In particular, it is necessary to isolate *absolute* change—i.e. those changing conditions on the PEP estate which it shares with its comparison estate—from *relative* change—i.e. those *additional* changes which were unique to the PEP estate and which might be attributed to the PEP intervention. It is also necessary to adjust statistically the estimates of relative change to correct for possible bias due to the inexact matching of experimental and control groups which occurs in the absence of random assignment. A description of the methodological rationale adopted and the survey research instruments used is contained in Appendix 1 of this volume. Appendix 2 outlines the methods employed and the ethnographic evaluation.

2 Crime prevention and the 'problem' estate

Why should the PEP model be expected to have an impact on crime? Although reductions in crime have been attributed to PEP (Chapter 1), it is not itself the embodiment of any particular theory of crime prevention but rather an initiative originating from a set of practical concerns about the management of public housing. Nevertheless, the role which the PEP model might play in controlling crime is worth investigation for two reasons: first, because the type of estate on which it is implemented is generally likely to exhibit a concentration of crime and social problems alongside its housing management ones; and second, because the PEP model may engender various changes in the physical and social character of estates which criminological research suggests might have an impact on crime. This chapter will describe this rationale in more detail.

The concentration of crime

The residents of council estates which are poor, both in the quality of their environments and in the circumstances of their inhabitants, are also likely to be victimised from crime to a greater extent than residents of other types of neighbourhood. Analysis of the 1988 British Crime Survey shows that households in council tenure face over twice the risk of burglary of those in owner occupation—92 compared with 44 burglaries or attempted burglaries per 1000 households (weighted data). The greater crime risk faced by council tenants has more to do with their residential concentration on housing estates than with tenure itself—tenants who live in areas where council tenure does not predominate have a risk of burglary only around the national average (Hope and Hough, 1988).

Crime risk is further concentrated *within* the council sector. The British Crime Survey shows that households in council tenure living in areas of majority council tenure and with the highest levels of poverty (as identified by the ACORN classification of the 1981 Census), face a risk of burglary around *five times* greater than tenants who live in areas where council housing is not the majority tenure and where tenants are better-off (Hope and Hough, 1988). Comparison between the same groups reveals that twice the proportion of residents of these 'poor council areas' are 'very worried' about becoming a victim of burglary in the coming year (Hope, 1986).

Two other features of this comparison are also noteworthy: first, proportionately twice as many residents of the poorer council areas say that problems such as graffiti, litter, noise from neighbours, disturbances from

5

teenagers, and so on, are very common in their neighbourhoods (Hope, 1986). In the eyes of residents, at least, there is a coincidence of crime problems with other forms of disorderly public behaviour (Skogan, 1990). Second, significantly more residents believe that most burglaries are committed by fellow residents—52 per cent compared to 29 per cent of council tenants living in non-council areas (Hope, 1986). In support of this latter view, research in British cities suggests a strong correlation between the proportion of known offenders in residential areas (the offender rate) and their rates of victimisation (the offence rate), with the highest rates of both falling within the council sector (Bottoms and Wiles, 1986). Offenders living in poorer areas are also more likely to offend in areas of similar or lesser social status, particularly their own (Davidson, 1984).

Finally, further analyses of the British Crime Survey show that, overall, the victims of most offences are concentrated in relatively few residential areas (Barr and Pease, 1990) and, particularly, that the victims of the more serious offences—such as theft from the person, robbery and burglary—are more likely to be found in 'inner city' areas, including the poorest council estates (Hope and Hough, 1988). In sum, the residents of these areas face a greater risk of being victimised from crime, particularly in the home environment, than people living elsewhere (Hough and Mayhew, 1985) and a disproportionate amount of all known victimisation occurs there. This increased risk generally goes hand in hand with a greater incidence of other disorders such as vandalism, litter, graffiti and a greater probability that those responsible also live in the same area. Thus, both to relieve the burden of crime for these residents and to reduce the level of victimisation overall, there is merit in targeting crime preventive action on the poorest council estates (see also Forrester *et al.*, 1990, 1988; Sampson and Farrell, 1990).

The concentration of housing management problems

The Priority Estates Project originated from concern about the concentration of housing management problems on particular estates. By the mid-1970s, the Department of the Environment had become concerned about a growing number of unpopular or difficult-to-let estates—sometimes ones that had been completed only relatively recently—and initiated a detailed study to investigate the problem (DoE, 1981). The investigation concluded that some estates acquire an adverse reputation which, when combined with an inability to maintain them to an adequate standard, results in a spiral of decline characterised by vandalised and poorly-maintained public spaces, no sense of community, and the departure of the more self-sufficient tenants by way of transfers to more desirable estates. As a consequence, there was a high turnover of tenants and vacancies which arose were attractive only to those in desperate housing need who, once housed, found it difficult to move on again. An atmosphere of neglect grew up making it even harder for housing services to cope with increasing problems of maintenance, lettings and rent arrears.

The means to tackle the problem was seen to lie in two related initiatives. The first of these was intensive decentralisation of housing management and services to the level of the estate itself. Housing services—repairs, caretaking and cleaning, rent collection, etc.—could then be focused with a greater degree of effort and co-ordination to come to grips with the condition of the estates, to implement improvements and to maintain them so that problems did not become overwhelming again (Power, 1984). This philosophy of decentralisation represented a conscious attempt to reverse post-war trends in the management of public housing and to rediscover the localised, face-to-face approach advocated by the early pioneers of social housing (Power, 1987b). While the architectural design and urban location of some estates created particular problems (cf. Newman, 1973; Coleman, 1985), the evidence showed similar problems on both older estates of houses (DoE, 1981, Volume 3) and new estates of flats (DoE, 1981, Volume 2). Neither were these problems peculiar to 'inner city' estates as they could be found with equal and sometimes greater magnitude on peripheral estates on the outskirts of cities (Centre for Environmental Studies, 1984). An emphasis on management seemed to be more generally applicable to the variety of problem estates.

The second important ingredient in changing the condition of the problem estate was seen as the involvement of tenants in its management. In this respect, PEP is part of an approach to community development on problem estates stretching back at least to the 1970s (Rock, 1988). The consultants involved in the development of PEP drew on the experience of initiatives by the National Association for the Care and Resettlement of Offenders (Hedges *et al.*, 1980; Bright and Petterson, 1984), and on work with tenants' organisations and housing co-operatives, to fashion an approach which rested on consultation with tenants on all aspects of estate improvements and the creation of ways in which they would be able to become involved in the direct management of estates.

The idea was that involved tenants would develop a greater stake in their estates and would act as a constant pressure on housing management to maintain conditions. In recent years the Government's policy has sought to increase the power of tenants in several ways, for example 'Tenants' Choice' legislation and the availability of new grants to aid the development of tenant-led initiatives. PEP has always pressed for at least a representative 'estate forum' as a consultative and advisory body (Glennerster and Turner, 1991) and has recently developed the Estate Management Board concept in which a partnership of tenants and council residents contract to manage an estate.

The concentration of social problems

The 1987 *General Household Survey*—conducted in the year in which this research study was started—also provided some evidence of the increasing

7

concentration of social disadvantage in council housing. As a whole, council tenants were becoming relatively poorer than those in other tenures. While in 1981 the mean gross weekly income of economically active heads of household who rented from the council was about three-quarters of that of economically active heads nationally, by 1987 their income had fallen to just over half the national figure. Similarly, the proportion of economically inactive heads of household in council tenure increased by just under a third between 1981 and 1987. A range of other indicators drawn from official statistics indicate a long-term change in the social profile of council tenants towards poorer households and other groups with specific needs such as the elderly, families on income support and single parent (usually female-headed) households (Forrest and Murie, 1990).

Commentators on housing issues have pointed to this trend as one of potential 'residualisation' of public housing—a movement towards a service which more often provides a safety net for those who cannot find suitable provision within the private sector. Most acknowledge this process to be a long-term combination of successive governments' housing policies—affecting the public sector, private rental and owner occupation—and demographic and economic change. Similar trends are occurring in other countries, for example, France (Willmott and Murie, 1988). The process has not reached the stage found, for example, in the United States, and since local authorities still own a quarter of the UK housing stock it is unlikely that residualisation will occur to the extent found there for many years, if ever. Nevertheless, the changing profile of public housing towards a concentration of the more economically-vulnerable groups represents a backdrop against which estate-based initiatives need to be seen.

The significance for the present study of a potential social 'polarisation' with respect to council tenure is that it may interact with the polarisation which occurs *within* the council sector—a process, apparent for many years (cf Wilson, 1963)—which can lead to a concentration of disadvantaged people being housed in low-status and low-quality council housing. Wilmott and Murie (1988), for instance, suggest that whatever the procedure adopted by housing officials for grading prospective tenants in terms of housing priority, queues of differing lengths will build up for particular types of dwelling or particular estates—the most popular or desirable estates having the longest queues. Those most in need of housing—especially the homeless—can least afford to wait and will more readily join the fastest moving queue which, by definition, will be for the least popular estates. Those who can wait—particularly established tenants seeking transfers—will be able to hold out for dwellings on the most desirable estates.

In general, research suggests that social polarisation between estates will occur, first, if there are real or perceived differences in quality between estates which affect their desirability in the eyes of prospective tenants and, second,

8

if there are social or behavioral differences between people which are related to their differing priorities for being rehoused. The process is also affected by fluctuations over time in the availability of public housing—affecting the choice between estates and the length and speed of their respecctive queues—and in demand—affecting the mix of people eligible or expecting to be housed. Finally, councils' allocation rules and practices may introduce additional effects by, for example, operating different priority criteria for new tenants and existing tenants seeking transfers or specific policies for housing particular groups—e.g. families with children, the homeless, the disabled, etc.. (Willmott and Murie, 1988).

In short, the varying combinations of these and other allocation considerations over time make it difficult to predict the long-term 'careers' of individual estates. Nevertheless, in as much as certain types of tenant come to be seen, rightly or wrongly, by other types of tenant as undesirable to live alongside, and the former come to be concentrated on estates perceived to be the least desirable, then, in addition to the other processes noted above, polarisation will itself become self-fuelling, until there is a significant change of circumstances. PEP has a potential to change these circumstances by upgrading the quality of estates to make them more desirable and attractive to a broader range of tenants and by local estate management control over lettings (Power, 1987b).

Recent debates about the existence, nature and possible causes of an 'underclass' in Britain and other countries have revolved around whether there are people whose poverty is accompanied by certain forms of behaviour—particularly, inability or unwillingness to participate in the workforce, not forming or sustaining families and involvement in crime and drug use (Smith, 1992). One aspect of this debate is whether a concentration of the poor (and the departure of better-off residents) in particular communities removes those sources of leadership, support and control which would otherwise keep deviant and crimimal activity in check (Wilson, 1987) and whether concentration of underclass members have deleterious consequences for communal life in those communities (Murray, 1990). An additional question, then, about social polarisation within the council sector, in the context of polarisation between tenures, is whether the process leads to the concentration of social problems on particular estates.

In sum, a range of evidence points to a coincident concentration of crime, housing management and social problems in the types of estate in which PEP usually works, meriting a similar concentration of preventive effort. However, to justify a specific crime prevention interest in PEP, it is still necessary to hypothesise how the PEP model might affect crime specifically; here, a range of criminological research can highlight the various possible ways which might serve as a set of propositions to guide the subsequent evaluative research.

9

Crime and control on the 'problem' estate

Generally, research shows that it is very difficult to describe the sequences of cause and effect linking the deterioration—or regeneration—of urban neighbourhoods to changes in their crime levels, because their many adverse characteristics are likely to interact over time in the process of decline—or removal (Skogan, 1990; Hope and Shaw, 1988; Taylor and Gottfredson, 1986; Taub *et al.*, 1984). As Bottoms and Wiles (1986) suggest, in order to unravel the inter-relationship between the various possible causal factors, explanations may also be needed of the *internal dynamics* of community change on estates—in other words, a chart of the 'crime career' of particular estates over time. The following paragraphs describe some of the factors which criminological research has suggested might shape a community's internal dynamics in the direction of either more social control or greater disorder.

Defensible space and dwelling security

Upgrading the security of dwellings is quite common in PEP schemes, often arising from consultation with tenants. Security improvements on estates can be made to individual dwellings—usually programmes to install better quality locks on windows and doors (see Allatt, 1984a)—or to blocks of dwellings, usually in the form of entry-phone systems or concierges (Safe Neighbourhoods Unit, 1985). The idea of redesigning the immediate dwelling environment in order to create more 'defensible space' (Newman, 1973) over which residents can more easily and effectively exert supervision and control has been subject to considerable research (for reviews see Mayhew, 1977; Taylor *et al.*, 1980) and has also had a fair degree of popularity with local housing authorities and tenants since the 1970s. Similar ideas have been implemented in a number of PEP schemes.

Part of the difficulty in assessing the impact of these environmental measures of crime prevention lies in deciding whether they operate directly on offenders' perception—by blocking or removing opportunities for crime—or whether they affect offenders indirectly by influencing or supporting residents in exercising greater control and supervision, the latter being that which serves as an eventual deterrent to offenders (see Rosenbaum, 1988a; Heal and Laycock, 1988). Reliable evidence of the effects of physical improvements on council estates is relatively scarce though there is some evidence that security improvements can enhance tenants' levels of satisfaction with their estate, and reduce their fear of crime, despite a limited impact on crime itself (Allat, 1984b). Nevertheless, while physical measures may enhance residents' security in their homes they may be of limited effectiveness if residents' feelings of safety on their estates are being undermined in other ways: for example, effective entry phone schemes in blocks of dwellings seem to depend upon the active support of residents to keep them operational, which can be

10

undermined, for instance, if residents are afraid of their neighbours *within* their block who are obviously not deterred by the system (Safe Neighbourhoods Unit, 1985).

It is also doubtful whether the degree of security usually added to dwellings on council estates is sufficient to resist most burglars, particularly if they may fear no other kind of action or reprisal from residents or others (cf. Allatt, 1984a; Mayhew, 1984). In sum, the research evidence tends to suggest that security and design changes alone may have less impact than when they act in conjunction with other aspects of local life which might be helping to promote greater community control over the residential environment (Taylor and Gottfredson, 1986; Hope, 1986b).

Maintaining a safe neighbourhood

A safe neighbourhood is not necessarily free from any kind of crime or misbehaviour whatsoever—perhaps a utopian ideal—but arguably one where there is at least a general expectation of a level of safety and orderliness which is sufficient for residents to live and to conduct their affairs in the home or on the streets without fear of predation from others. Safety has both an objective and subjective component: the actual risk of crime and the way in which people adapt to what they believe to be their risk. The relevance of the subjective aspect of safety is best illustrated in how people react to its perceived absence—for example, fear of going outside the dwelling, desire to move to another area, lack of satisfaction with or participation in the community, stress, and so on (cf. Skogan *et al.*, 1982; Taylor and Hale, 1986). Together, these reactions—which are usually more visible than crime itself—impoverish the quality of life for residents and diminish its atractiveness to others (Skogan, 1988a). Thus, the perceived absence of safety is an issue for public policy both as something which affects the well-being of individuals and also as something which, in aggregate, has damaging consequences for the social and economic fabric of residential neighbourhoods (Hope and Shaw, 1988).

The most potent source of a sense of insecurity is being a victim of crime but even on the highest crime estates it is unlikely that everyone will be victimised constantly and some crime experiences may be much less worrying to some people than others. Nevertheless, a general sense of insecurity can also build-up from a variety of *indirect* experiences of crime and disorder, including witnessing incidents and hearing about the victimisation of others, particularly of friends, relations and neighbours (Skogan and Maxfield, 1981). Each individual victimisation resounds through contacts between family, friends and neighbours and, if residents are unhappy about other aspects of the quality of life, crime can come to symbolise the general ills of their neighbourhood (Taub *et al.*, 1984). For instance, almost twice as many tenants in the poorest, compared with the better-off, council areas personally know someone whose home has been burgled in the past year, and four times

11

as many tenants (13 per cent) spontaneously mention crime as the 'worst thing about living in their area' (Hope, 1986). If PEP can restore a sense of confidence amongst residents, it may strengthen their resistance to crime.

The presence of litter, graffiti, vandalism and general environmental decay is closely related to residents' worries about crime and safety and these 'signs of disorder' are an everyday reminder of insecurity within the neighbourhood (Skogan, 1988a). Since PEP schemes almost always focus initially on cleaning-up the estate, speeding-up the letting of empty dwellings and effecting general repairs, they may also promote a greater feeling of safety by removing the most visible signs of disorder (Power, 1989). At face value, these activities might appear to be simply cosmetic but there are grounds for thinking that the removal of signs of disorder could have beneficial long-term consequences for the general safety of the estate.

A number of commentators have taken the strong relationships found between signs of disorder, fear of crime, community dissatisfaction and victimisation itself (for which see Skogan, 1990; Hope and Hough, 1988) as an indication of a general spiral of decline which visible disorders can accelerate (Hope and Shaw, 1988). Wilson and Kelling (1982) make use of the analogy of 'broken windows'—failure to rectify damage and deterioration can give powerful cues to would-be offenders that nobody cares about the neighbourhood and no one is likely to intervene or take action to prevent crime. They had in mind police strategies to enforce orderly conduct on the streets but PEP's efforts to provide estate-based repair teams represent a literal belief in the value of stemming vandalism before it comes to be seen as a defining characteristic of a difficult-to-let estate. The expectation is that a well-maintained estate becomes the outward and visible sign of care and concern, encouraging in residents a greater sense of pride in their residential area and support for efforts to preserve safety and orderliness.

A more contentious set of disorders are those seen as attaching to people (Skogan, 1990). Certain types of activity or behaviour in public—teenagers hanging around, groups of people drinking in public—or in the home environment—noisy neighbours and loud parties—are associated with a higher degree of fear and worry about crime, particularly for older people and urban residents and especially those in the poorest council estates (Maxfield, 1987a). Reynolds' (1986) study of a problem estate found disputes and dissatisfaction with neighbours a common reason for dissatisfaction with the estate as a whole. The opening of a local housing office on the estate may provide a more accessible means for worried tenants to gain support, remedy or redress. Control over lettings by local housing management can provide greater opportunities to enforce legal agreements with disorderly tenants and, in being closer to the estate, local officers can more easily use a variety of informal methods to mediate differences between neighbours. In this sense, a local management presence—including resident caretakers—might help underpin a greater degree of order and regulation in tenant relations. Finally, PEP improvements can provide a greater opportunity for effective community policing. Council estates often present particular problems for beat policing in terms of regular access to the estate not just by virtue of their design (Newman, 1972) but also legally as communal 'semi- public' areas are often the private property of the council (Osborn and Bright, 1988). Together, these factors can encourage a very reactive style with the police only coming onto the estate in response to calls for assistance. In contrast, the local office on a PEP estate can provide a focus and more informal opportunity for the police to visit the estate. Contact with a representative tenants' organisation can provide the invitation for the police to patrol the estate on a regular basis—indeed, a greater police presence and involvement on the estate is often one of the first requests of tenants in a PEP scheme (Power, 1989). PEP might thus act as a facilitator for improved police-community relations and for more effective patrolling and home beat policing.

Investing in the estate

The image of the problem estate is one where most residents have little stake in their community and their strongest desire is to move away. People's attachment to the place where they live can be both instrumental—i.e. the value which the housing market and they themselves attach to the amenities of the area—and affective—i.e. the value they attach to living alongside their neighbours. In respect of instrumental values, the foregoing discussion has identified low-demand as one of the key characteristics of the problem estate. To the extent that PEP improves conditions—for example, by cleaning up the estate, it can raise the estate's value in the eyes of current and prospective residents. By creating a cleaner and safer environment it can revive estate amenities—such as playgrounds, car parks and shopping areas—which had fallen into disuse and it can provide new amenities of value—such as secure dwellings or a local office convenient for paying the rent, etc. Residents of communities where the value of the amenities and the housing stock is rising are more likely to have lower levels of fear and a greater degree of confidence and commitment than residents of areas with comparable crime levels but whose value is declining (Taub *et al.*, 1984). Visible signs of positive investment in the estate may strengthen the community to resist the growth of crime and this can have beneficial long-term consequences.

Community control

PEP places considerable emphasis on fostering representative tenant organisations and providing them with the means to play a greater role in the every-day management of their estates. In general this can mean participation in day-to-day decisions about estate management and maintenance and acquiring support and facilities for community amenities and organisations. Specifically, PEP might encourage three developments: first, by bringing people together in organisations or through shared amenities, it may foster the growth of informal *neighbourliness* which is the bedrock of community life (Abrams, 1986). Neighbourliness is an important way in which people develop affective attachments to the place where they live. Second, through the work of representative tenant organisations there may grow a sense of *'neighbourhood-ism'* (Abrams, 1986)—the development of a shared identity amongst residents about their estate. This can lead to a greater sense of *empowerment*—a belief in the ability of a community to solve its problems collectively through its own efforts and to mobilise other agencies to help them. Third, community development can lead to the longer-term establishment of community *institutions*—e.g. parent-and-toddler and pre-school play groups, youth clubs, old people's lunch clubs, parent-teacher associations etc.—which can outlast the tenure of their founding members and become part of the fabric of the community. Nevertheless, as noted below, community development efforts may themselves depend upon a certain prior degree of community cohesion and consensus, which may be lacking in high crime communities.

The relevance of PEP's community development efforts for crime prevention is that they might foster the greater effectiveness of *informal social control* (Greenberg *et al.*, 1985). The possibility that local communities can exert their own informal control over offending within their midst has been a recurring theme in criminological research (Reiss, 1988) and studies have found forms of control operating in many different kinds of neighbourhood alongside formal policing (Shapland and Vagg, 1988). Contemporary understanding of this idea takes two broad forms: in the first place, informal social control can be exerted in the form of *surveillance* over the residential environment, a concept shared both by 'neighbourhood watch' and 'defensible space'. '[T]he primary objective is the same, whether the intervention is social or physical: namely, to reduce the *opportunity* for criminal activity in specific settings by increasing the risk of detection and apprehension' (Rosenbaum, 1988a, p. 328). In this definition, control relies upon the possibility of residents intervening to forestall crimes from taking place, either personally or, more usually, by calling the police. PEP has the potential for fostering surveillance through defensible space modifications, through the neighbourliness encouraged by its community development activities, or through the presence of housing officials (including caretakers) to whom incidents can be reported.

Another meaning of informal control is the idea of a community upholding its own norms of conduct and regulating its members to abide by such standards, for example, not to victimise people on the estate (despite, perhaps, involvement in crime elsewhere). In this sense, social control consists of rewards or sanctions that members of a community can invoke to ensure their own and other members' conformity to these standards. Common sanctions might typically be the withholding of esteem or exclusion from social activities, though physical actions and the reporting of violators' misbehaviour and abuses to the housing department, social services or the police are also possible. Standards are upheld through a range of actions including verbal reprimands, gossip and less subtle threats (Greenberg *et al.*, 1985). Again, while the growth of neighbourliness that PEP might foster provides a means of expressing control it is probably necessary for a broader community identity to prevail for individuals to have confidence that others will support their actions in upholding standards of conduct. In the long-term, it is also possible that collective participation in community institutions will help to maintain standards of behaviour, particularly with regard to raising young people (Kornhauser, 1978). Whatever their preferred remedies, the basic desirability of fostering informal community control over local offending is shared by writers from a broad spectrum of opinion (cf. Wilson, 1975; Currie, 1988).

Population change

There may also be sociological factors which reinforce and sustain the activities of offenders in residential communities. Of particular importance is the role of *population change*—which in the public housing context is a function of the operation of local authority tenant allocation decisions made within the constraints of the local housing market. Most of the foregoing discussion has pointed to the way in which PEP might help to facilitate informal community control over crime. Yet, as in many discussions of community crime prevention, there is an implicit tendency to assume that a latent 'community' of residents already exists which only needs some help to express itself—something which cannot necessarily be taken for granted (see Skogan, 1988b; Rosenbaum, 1988b). Criminologists have noted that high crime communities may be socially and culturally heterogeneous (Kornhauser, 1978; Shaw and McKay, 1969). As Power (1989) found from first-hand experience, there are often deep divisions amongst the residents of the estates on which PEP works—a finding common to many community studies of poorer neighbourhoods over the years, and particularly of council estates (Reynolds, 1986). Though such divisions may derive from differences in income or race (cf. Merry, 1981), tenants may also distinguish amongst themselves in terms of lifestyle or aspirations, even amongst those with similar economic prospects (Parker, 1983). Such divisions may make it harder to organise tenants across the estate into co-operative crime prevention initiatives because the necessary prerequisite of community cohesion is lacking (Skogan, 1988b).

Social divisions amongst tenants—and changes in the social mix on estates—may also have a more direct bearing on criminal activity itself. There are a number of ways in which this might happen: in the first place, in as much as some families within a community may be more willing to engage in criminal or anti-social behaviour than others, their presence, in the absence of any restraining influences, may 'cause problems out of all proportion to their actual numbers' (Cullingworth quoted in Power, 1989). Additionally, a concentration of families where parents exercise little supervision over their boys' behaviour (Wilson, 1980), or who are unaware of how their children spend their leisure time (Riley and Shaw, 1985), may lead to the emergence of groups of unsupervised teenagers on estates who may in turn engage in vandalism and other delinquency (Wilson, 1982). Second, frequent and rapid turnover of tenants may be destabilising and inhibit the formation of informal relations and institutions, the absence of which (as noted above) may inhibit the ability of the community to regulate crime—a process of 'social disorganisation' which has been of considerable interest to criminologists for many years (Reiss, 1986). Third, the concentration of disadvantaged families on particular estates may lead young people especially, in the face of adversity and with little prospect of change, to see the apparent gains from criminal activities and lifestyles as an irresistible temptation (see Wilson, 1987; Sullivan, 1989). Such attractions may lead to the emergence of criminal networks of various kinds within poor communities.

A change in the *rate* of turnover is not sufficient in itself to bring about change in crime levels. Comparative research in residential areas of Sheffield found high crime estates with high tenant turnovers—supporting a social disorganisation explanation of crime. (Bottoms and Wiles, 1986). In estates with low tenant turnover, the criminality of the estate seemed to have been reinforced by its residential *stability*, leading to the long-term maintenance of networks of families and friends with criminal interests, into which younger generations were recruited (Bottoms *et al.*, 1989). This latter process can lead over time to the reinforcement of offending networks into which successive cohorts are recruited and through which members evolve different modes of offending as they mature (Foster, 1990).

Research into patterns of neighbourhood change in Britain and the USA suggests that sudden changes in the rate of turnover or in the type of new arrival can have quite dramatic destabilising effects, leading neighbourhoods to 'tip' into spirals of deterioration or, sometimes, renewal (see Hope, 1986b). Implicitly, PEP's diagnosis of crime on the problem estate is that of 'social disorganisation' (Power, 1989). Once stability is achieved, community motivation and organisation can be built-up to attain more effective internal controls over remaining criminal activity within the estate. The successful implementation of the PEP model may thus also help reinforce community stability by encouraging existing tenants to stay, halting a headlong flight from the estate and thus regulating the pace at which new residents arrive, hopefully helping with their integration into the estate community.

Conclusions

The ways in which the research literature suggests how PEP might reduce crime, which have been described in the foregoing sections, can be summarised by the model presented at Figure 1 overleaf. The core assumption of this model is that crime and incivility are affected by residents' ability to exert informal control over behaviour on their estates. PEP may stimulate the growth of control by giving tenants a stake in their community, a feeling of empowerment about influencing affairs on their estates, and an optimism about the future. A sense of community control can be translated into practical action by measures to assist residents' ability to supervise behaviour on their estates, including the better opportunities for surveillance afforded by environmental modifications and the greater accessibility of estate-based housing officials and police, to whom problems can be reported. In the longer-run, such actions may be sustained through the support and encouragement of emerging community groups and organisations. Key steps in the growth of social control are the development of positive valuations by residents' of their estates (Hope, 1986b) and the encouragement of involvement in activity beyond their front doors—whether informal concern about behaviour in their residential environment ('natural surveillance') or more active involvement in community organisations and in the management of the estate ('institution-building').

Figure 1: Model of Priority Estates Project effect on crime

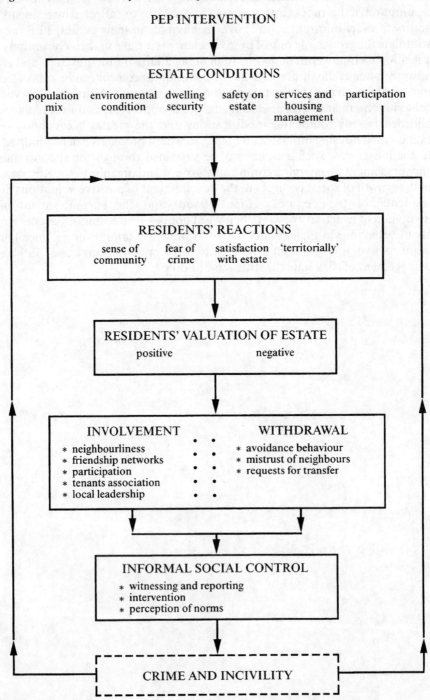

PEP INTERVENTION

ESTATE CONDITIONS

| population mix | environmental condition | dwelling security | safety on estate | services and housing management | participation |

RESIDENTS' REACTIONS

| sense of community | fear of crime | satisfaction with estate | 'territorially' |

RESIDENTS' VALUATION OF ESTATE

positive   negative

INVOLVEMENT

* neighbourliness
* friendship networks
* participation
* tenants association
* local leadership

WITHDRAWAL

* avoidance behaviour
* mistrust of neighbours
* requests for transfer

INFORMAL SOCIAL CONTROL

* witnessing and reporting
* intervention
* perception of norms

CRIME AND INCIVILITY

The contribution of the PEP model to reducing crime lies in its potential for encouraging residents' collective, informal control over behaviour on their estates. Though not an explicit aim, a case has been made here for seeing PEP as an attempt to 'implant' crime control into estate communities (Rosenbaum, 1988). Nevertheless, as with other attempts to implant informal control (Skogan, 1990), the extent to which PEP can be seen to be making a *unique* contribution may depend upon other factors which affect community cohesion. The most important of these are the changes which occur in the social mix of estates over time. Changes in the rate of population turnover, and in the kinds of people entering or leaving the estate, can affect the cohesion and stability of estate communities in ways which may enhance or undermine community members' capacity to influence informal control.

Population change on council housing estates is shaped, in complex ways, by local housing departments' practices in allocating their housing stock to current and prospective tenants. The extent to which housing departments can in practice influence the social mix and stability of their estate communities depends upon the amount of leeway they have at their disposal in reconciling their various statutory responsibilities and social obligations to provide housing with the stock of dwellings they have available at any particular time. Wider changes in the overall housing market—particularly social polarisation between tenures and within the public housing sector—will considerably influence housing departments' scope for manoeuvre, especially their ability to radically change the position of unpopular estates within the housing market. Yet these constraints may also affect the capacity of PEP to bring about change on estates. As will be seen in subsequent chapters of this report, the success of the PEP model depends *both* upon how it is implemented on specific estates *and* on the operation of other factors simultaneously affected changes in the social mix of the estates.

3 Community and crime on the estates

Four estates were studied with varying degrees of intensity over the three year period between June 1987 and July 1990. As explained in Chapter 1, the evaluation research design called for two new PEP estates each to be paired with a comparison or 'control' estate. Within practical constraints, an attempt was made to find two different kinds of new PEP estate and to match them with relatively similar control estates from within the same local housing authority. This chapter describes and compares the estates prior to the initiation of the first PEP in 1987.

The estates

1. *The London experimental estate*

The London experimental estate was located in the London Borough of Tower Hamlets and comprised two large, modern, system-built, deck-access blocks opened in 1971 (214 units); a block of flats erected in 1957; a small number of three storey houses; an area separated by a main road which was composed of several blocks built between 1936 and 1960, and a scattering of flats and houses. Though administered as a single unit, differences in design, physical layout and the fact that one part of the estate was formerly managed by the Greater London Council (GLC) while the other was run by the Borough did not encourage an estate-wide identity.

2. *The Hull experimental estate*

The Hull PEP estate contrasted markedly with the London experimental site and was more 'typical' of the estates which PEP have tackled in the past. The estate was part of a much larger council housing development—about 3,500 dwellings—built during the 1960s on the outskirts of the city. The part of the development which formed the experimental estate contained 1,083 properties; half of these were houses (514) with the remainder divided between four high rise blocks of flats, three nine or ten storey blocks and a few three-storey 'town houses' (569 properties in total). With the exception of some of the tower blocks, the estate in 1987 was not divided into tangible and distinct areas. Tenants were aware that they were only a small part of the much larger housing development and there were few boundaries to distinguish one part of the estate from another. Two features of the estate's design were noteworthy: first, the estate was planned according to the 'Radburn' principle of ensuring maximum segregation of vehicles and pedestrians. In practice, this meant having a road around the periphery of the estate from which feeder roads led-off, expanses of open space around the blocks of flats, and houses connected by pedestrian walkways and courtyards, often opening directly onto pathways. Second, the houses were constructed using a pre-cast concrete, system method, which were difficult to heat cheaply and, over time, subject to excessive condensation. There were practically no private areas on the estate, the grey pebble dash houses 'crammed cheek-by-jowl into terraces' (from an independent consultants' report to the local authority) set out in monotonous rows which many tenants often likened to 'army barracks'. The houses had no front gardens and people could walk freely from one part of the estate to another.

3. *The London control estate*

Like the London experimental estate, the London control estate contained a mixture of property types. The estate consisted of three tower blocks (1968/70), two modern balcony access blocks with linked walkways (1965 and 1977), a few bungalows and houses (1968) and one walk-up balcony block (1938). Like its counterpart, this estate had been formerly administered by the now-defunct GLC. Close by, a separate area consisted of three balcony blocks (1954) which had always been managed by the Borough of Tower Hamlets.

4. *The Hull control estate*

Like the experimental estate, the control estate formed part of a larger area also located on the outskirts of the city, at one time reputed to be the biggest public housing development in Western Europe. The estate was also laid out to Radburn principles and the houses constructed with no-fines materials. Nevertheless, most of the houses had front gardens and although 30 per cent of dwellings were flats, they were contained in two-storey blocks.

The estates compared in 1987

Tables 1a and 1b overleaf compare the social profiles of the estate populations as measured by the first survey in July 1987. All the estates had large proportions of poor, non-working residents. Generally, the pairs of estates were matched relatively well, though there were some exceptions. First, there were, for instance, more single people on both the PEP estates than on their control estates. Second, the London experimental estate in particular had a lower ethnic minority population than its control estate, and the ethnic mix differed—on the control estate, minorities were predominantly of Indian sub-continental origin, particularly Bangladeshi (27 per cent), while ethnic minority groups were much more evenly balanced on the experimental estate, including Afro-Caribbeans and Cantonese/Vietnamese (9 per cent). Third, the Hull estates had, on the whole more children, fewer people working and were poorer than the London estates. Finally, the London estates, especially the experimental estate, at the outset took a much higher proportion of its incoming residents from those in various forms of housing need—e.g. homelessness, medical reasons—than in Hull, reflecting a greater pressure on public housing in the capital.

Table 1a
Demographic profiles of survey respondents from the four estates (1987)—individuals

	Hull		London	
	PEP	control	PEP	control
persons aged 60 plus yrs (%)	24	20	23	25
children under 16 yrs (%)	24	24	10	11
married or cohabiting (%)	48	38	50	37
persons in full or part-time work (%)	25	30	34	35
Asian[1] (%)	1	0	7	30
Vietnamese[2] (%)	0	0	9	0
Afro-Caribbean[3] (%)	1	0	10	4
BASE (individuals)	578	480	242	382

Weighted data.
Notes:
[1]Persons describing themselves as: Bangladeshi, Indian, Pakistani, or UK/British Asian.
[2]Persons describing themselves as: Chinese or Vietnamese.
[3]Persons describing themselves as: Caribbean/West Indian, African or UK/British Black.

Table 1b
Demographic profiles of survey respondents from the four estates (1987)—household characteristics

	Hull		London	
	PEP	control	PEP	control
households with children (%)	30	40	14	15
persons per household	2.43	2.91	2.14	2.21
single parent households (%)	5	4	3	3
single adult households (%)	21	10	17	16
households owning one or more motor vehicles (%)	38	40	45	33
households in owner-occupation (%)	2	10	6	4
households receiving housing benefit (%)	39	35	27	26
households in Social Class E[1] (%)	53	49	47	43
households resident less than 3 years (%)	36	29	29	26
percentage of new households from outside council sector[2]	48	45	87	59
BASE: (households)	578	480	242	382

Weighted data.
Notes:
[1]State pensioners, widows (no other earners), casual or lowest grade workers, long term unemployed.
[2]Percentage of households resident on estate less than three years who moved to the estate from the housing waiting list, from homelessness, compulsory purchase or for other reasons (including medical).

Estate problems

Table 2 shows that in general the residents of all the estates shared many of the dissatisfactions typically associated with problem estates. The relatively lower proportions of residents on the London estates who thought their estate had a bad reputation among people who lived elsewhere in the borough may be due, in part, to the relatively greater anonymity of these smaller estates compared to larger problem estates in their local authority areas. Very high proportions of residents on the Hull estates thought their estates had bad reputations even though significant numbers still expressed satisfaction with their estates. On all but the Hull control estate, the majority of residents thought that their estates had got worse over the previous two years and appreciable numbers thought that their estates would continue to deteriorate. Not surprisingly, around half of all residents on each estate said they would move given the choice. The remainder of this chapter describes conditions on the two experimental estates prior to PEP starting work.

Table 2

Estate problems: critical features (survey responses—1987)

	Hull		London	
	PEP	control	PEP	control
estate has bad reputation in area (%)	86	73	43	26
very satisfied with estate (%)	62	53	47	60
estate has got worse over past 2 years (%)	63	49	65	67
estate will get worse in next 2 years (%)	32	57	53	40
would move if had the choice (%)	54	48	55	50
BASE (respondents)	578	480	242	382

Weighted data.

Crime: critical features

Table 3 shows that the Hull estates had far higher overall crime rates than the London estates—well above the national average even for comparable areas, as estimated from the 1984 British Crime Survey. Table 4 (on page 25) shows similar levels of worry between the two experimental estates about becoming a victim of a specific offence like burglary, vandalism or mugging. However, the ethnographic research revealed a far higher level of unease about crime in Hull than in London and, in particular, Table 4 shows that women on the Hull estate were far more worried about being raped or sexually assaulted on the estate than women on the London estate.

Table 3
Victimisation rates for household and personal offences
(compared with British Crime Survey 1984 rates)
Rate per 100 households

	Hull		London		British crime survey		
	PEP	control	PEP	control	all	Acorn[1]	
						G	FG
Household offences							
vandalism	34	26	16	16	16	17	17
theft from motor vehicle	11	16	14	10	7	11	8
burglary in dwelling	12	10	13	16	5	19	9
theft of motor vehicle	3	3	5	2	2	2	2
bicycle theft	4	6	1	0	1	4	3
theft in a dwelling	5	2	0	1	1	2	1
other household theft	29	33	12	15	9	20	13
TOTAL	98	94	60	61	41	75	53
Personal offences							
assault	8	11	4	7	5	8	6
theft from person/robbery	1	1	2	3	2	4	2
sexual offences	1	0	1	0	0	0	0
TOTAL	9	12	7	10	7	12	8
BASE (respondents)	578	480	242	382	10,640	543	1,718

Weighted data.

Notes:

1 ACORN is a neighbourhood classification system based on the 1981 Census. ACORN Group F is 'Council Estates—category II', ACORN Group G is 'Council Estates—category III'.

2 Rates constructed according to the same 'counting rules' as have been used with the British Crime Survey (Hough and Mayhew, 1985). This differs from that adopted subsequently in this report.

24

Table 4
Worry about crime and disorder
(survey responses—1987)

	Hull		London	
	PEP	*control*	*PEP*	*control*
percentage of respondents who were 'very worried' about:				
having home broken into and				
something stolen	55	41	59	65
having home or property damaged				
by vandals	57	41	57	66
being attacked or robbed while on				
the estate	56	45	60	65
being raped or sexually assaulted on				
the estate (asked of women only)	50	45	29	42
perception of estate problems (mean score index)[1]				
environmental incivilities[2]	198	169	158	144
person-related disorderliness[3]	152	133	130	118
broken windows and doors	170	135	164	162
percentage thinking that crime is worse on estate than on other estates in local authority area:				
BASE (respondents)	23	14	5	16

Weighted data.
Notes:
1 Responses to items were: 3 = 'big problem'; 2 = 'something of a problem'; 1 = 'not a problem'. The index was constructed by $100 (k/n)$, where k = sum of responses in the set and n = number of responses in set. A score of 100 = 'not a problem' for every item, a score of 300 = 'big problem' for every item.
2 Environmental incivilities include: lack of safe play spaces; rubbish and litter lying around; problems associated with dogs; graffiti; broken street lighting; empty houses/flats, inadequate secure car-parking; broken down and abandoned cars.
3 Person-related disorderliness includes: disturbances from teenagers and youths; noisy parties; noisy neighbours; noisy people outside the home; people mending vehicles outside the home; people insulting or bothering others in public; people using illegal drugs; speeding traffic; people hanging around drinking.

The disparity in crime rates between the two experimental estates was primarily due to higher rates of the more minor household offences—rates of burglary, and theft of or from motor vehicles were comparable and sometimes higher on the London estates. Nevertheless, incidents of petty crime and disorder (Chapter 2) impinge more frequently on people's lives than the more serious but rarer offences and this meant that crime was likely to play a greater part in the lives of residents on the Hull experimental estate than on the London estate. For instance, 43 per cent of households on the Hull experimental estate had been the victim of at least one household offence in the past year compared to 31 per cent on the London estate.

The greater everyday presence of crime and disorder in Hull as compared to London was also illustrated in the likelihood of residents witnessing different types of incidents. Table 5 shows that Hull residents were much more likely to have witnessed disorderly public behaviour, particularly involving teenagers, than London residents, while the proportions witnessing more serious crime incidents were about the same. As Table 4 shows, the generally greater level of disorderliness in Hull was reflected in the greater proportions of residents saying that a range of different types of disorder or incivility (see Chapter 2) were problems on their estate.

Table 5
Incidents personally seen or heard on estate in the last year—1987
(percentages)

	Hull PEP estate	London PEP estate
people dumping rubbish/litter	49	46
noise from neighbours	33	33
children/teens swearing in streets	84	53
children/teens damaging property	50	38
children/teens sniffing glue or using drugs	10	8
people fighting	51	33
children/teens hanging around	82	64
people drinking in street	57	26
someone threatening someone	36	21
someone breaking into a house/flat	12	18
someone breaking into car/van	12	13
someone being attacked or mugged	7	10
BASE (respondents)	578	242

There were a number of possible reasons why the Hull experimental estate appeared to have more petty crime and disorder than its London counterpart. In the first place, the greatest disparities between the Hull and London estates occurred in these offence categories—especially vandalism and 'other household theft'[1]—most commonly associated with younger teenagers (Gladstone, 1978)—and in the witnessing of disorders in which young people were involved (Table 5). There was a greater number of children and teenagers on the Hull estate (Table 1a, p22), hardly any play spaces or youth facilities and high rates of youth unemployment (a report in 1985 estimated that youth unemployment on the estate might have been as high as 80 per cent). The scale of the estate made it impossible for tenants to know the majority of youths personally, while the sheer volume of youths may have created a buffer from adult authority, there being 'safety in numbers'.

Some tenants on the Hull experimental estate tried, and on most occasions failed, to enforce control of the teenagers. Many tenants were fearful of these youths whose threats to break their windows or damage their property were taken seriously. This inhibited tenants intervening personally and in some cases prevented them reporting incidents to the police. On the occasions where the police were called tenants often felt that no effective action had resulted from their presence. Consequently troublesome youths seemed to have free rein to do as they pleased and no one appeared able to stop them. As one of the tenants commented: 'youths, they ran the estate, you daren't say anything to them. . . . The people in the houses daren't say anything to them, otherwise they get their windows put in, it was that kind of thing. So there was just plain anarchy, each of the people sort of took their family into their own house and defended their own property. That was their defensible area within the walls of the house. My family in here, I don't care what happens outside, which is the wrong thing to do of course.'

Secondly, the relative isolation of the London experimental estate (being surrounded on all sides by roads, two of them major roads) and its courtyard design, with the natural surveillance which this allows, may also have contributed to less concern about crime and public disorderliness. Different blocks and sections of the estate were regarded by the residents as separate territories. The architects of the two large blocks on the London experimental estate developed Le Corbusier's concept of 'streets in the sky' (cf Eisenham 1972) where the blocks would form 'a continuous elevated street network'. While this design can constrain the degree of surveillance, and allow a larger number of people access to the walkways than is perhaps desirable in terms of security, many tenants still used the balconies, chatted to their neighbours and passers-by and simply stood on the balcony to get out of their flats. The balcony actually performed an important social function contrary to, for example, Coleman's (1985) typification of what life in blocks of this kind might be like. In contrast, the size and open plan layout of the Hull experimental estate—with its warren of internal pathways accessible from all sides—resulted in a depressed sense of territoriality. As one of the tenants commented: 'it is wide open, is this estate . . . it's a burglar's paradise.' Another tenant said: 'this estate . . . was quite possibly one of the worst estates that had been planned'. Thus, the greater amount of public space on the Hull experimental estate, and the higher proportion of houses and garages, created more *opportunities* and *targets* for youthful petty crime and disorder.[1]

Third, prior to PEP's intervention, there were already reasonably established forms of informal and formal social control on the London experimental estate. The first tenants association, established in 1974, was formed in response to youths vandalising the estate. Tenants organised 'patrols' of the blocks to deter youths. These patrols were felt by residents to have contained youth problems on the estate and prevented the development of an intimidating youthful presence. Tenants continued to intervene if they witnessed criminal or anti-social acts. For example, not long before the start of the study, tenants had remonstrated with the children responsible for stealing items from the community club-room and confronted the parents of children caught adorning the lifts with graffiti.

---

[1] A category of household offences covering thefts and attempts from domestic garages, outhouses, sheds, etc. and thefts from outside the dwelling.

A home beat police officer had been assigned to the London experimental estate prior to PEP's involvement. She developed a good rapport with tenants and adopted both formal and informal sanctions to address the problems experienced by them. 'She really does put herself out' one of the tenants said, 'she seems like a friend now, whenever you see her she'll have a chat, how are you, how's the tenants association gettin' on?' The home beat officer's treatment of some illegal parties on the estate provides a good illustration of her approach. After arranging for a tenant to observe the flat over a period of weeks a raid was organised 'not because I could do anything specific to stop (the parties) but at least they thought I was doing something. That's quite an important thing.' Although the people involved were released without charge, the parties did in fact stop. Despite the high levels of crime on the Hull experimental estate there was no home beat officer assigned to the estate prior to PEP's intervention. Tenants had little confidence in the police. On the Hull estate, only 23 per cent of residents expressed any satisfaction with 'what the police are doing on the estate these days' compared to 45 per cent on the London estate; while 39 per cent thought there were less police patrolling the estate than two years previously, compared to 16 per cent in London.

Reputation and stigma

As described in Chapter 2, estates can acquire an adverse reputation which has a powerful influence on the way current and prospective residents, and others in the community, act towards them. Residents on both the London and Hull experimental estates had to contend with socially stigmatizing reactions.

On the London experimental estate, the ugly architectural design of the two system blocks, which dominated the area, seemed to be the primary source of the estate's reputation. One woman recollected how, when asking for directions to the estate, an old man commented 'oh you mean Alcatraz!' Certain architectural styles, particularly system-built estates, have come to be associated with social problems (see Coleman, 1985) yet there is always a possibility that an adverse reputation may evolve merely because of the stigma imputed to particular styles of design. In this case it appears that many judged the estate on its architectural appearance alone and made several other assumptions about the estate being a 'problem'. At the outset of the research it was common for housing staff to talk in emotive terms about issues like crime and racial harassment which occurred on the estate when these were in reality rather less of a problem than litter and the poor lift service.

Despite its ugly appearance, the estate was considered desirable by tenants when it opened in 1971, particularly in comparison with the dwellings that the new tenants had left behind. However, it did not take long for tenants' perceptions and the reputation of the estate to change. Long-term tenants believed that the estate changed as numbers of the original tenants moved out and 'different' tenants—i.e. single people, students and 'problem families'—moved in (cf Damer, 1974). There were differing perceptions about when this process began to occur but by the mid 70s, the estate had acquired a 'difficult to let' status and tenants who moved onto the estate just three or four years after it opened had negative views about it.

In the years preceding the start of the research, there had been a gradual rise in the number of ethnic minorities living on the estate. Vietnamese refugees were allocated flats there in the 1970s along with some Afro-Caribbean and Asian households. Around 26 per cent of respondents in the 1987 survey were of ethnic minority origin (Table 1a, p22). Amongst some white tenants, the ethnic minorities on the estate, especially the Bengalis, were a convenient group to blame for the estate's problems, for example:

> A lot of Bangladesh people ... they are a community amongst themselves. Their way of life is so caught up in their culture that I think even in a hundred years it's going to be so difficult to really encourage them and help them live in Britain as British people... There's so many problems... Women aren't supposed to go out on their own and... their lives are just so different from ours that you just can't start ... There is a lot of hostility. People generally in the East End [of London] are very racist. They don't like foreigners at all they don't want them here, they're not interested, they feel that they're the cause of all the problems.' (White tenant, London experimental estate, 1988).

The Hull experimental estate was originally constructed to relieve housing pressure created by slum clearance schemes in the city. A large number of the first inhabitants came from a particular area which had a notorious reputation; many prospective tenants from other parts of the city, it was said, had not wanted to live alongside what were deemed slum clearance families. Like Damer's Wine Alley (1974) the estate became inextricably linked with, and never recovered from, the stigma of slum clearance (see also Gill, 1977, Armstrong and Wilson, 1973). Many of the slum clearance families experienced extreme social isolation when they were rehoused on the estate. Nevertheless, as many of the new tenants came from inadequate housing, their initial reactions were often relatively favourable.

> This area was smashing for all those who ... were from the inner city who moved out here. It was like moving to the country because before this estate was built this was country, it was the boundaries of Hull ... it was a model estate ... brand new houses. Everybody had been used to back to backs, you know, terraced houses and it was different (up here). You had a garden, everything was large, plenty of room, plenty of cupboard space. It was like moving from rented accomodation to buying yer own house ... it was brand spanking new.

29

Those who had formed good community ties at the outset blamed the decline of the estate on successive 'different' or 'problem' tenants who did not share their values and attitudes. As the estate was designed for families, some women were able to establish links with other tenants on the estate of a similar age and experience (cf. Suttles, 1972; Abrams, 1986). Unfortunately as time went by, the geographical and social isolation, and the lack of community facilities—particularly for play and recreation for the large numbers of children—began to foster a sense of hopelessness: 'people gave up' a tenant explained 'at first we used to see them come out and scrub their fronts, kept them nice and clean and I think they just gave up after a few years.'

The estate became one of the least in demand in Hull and it was often only the most desperate and needy who would accept offers of housing there. According to a report by consultants to the City Council, the social and economic characteristics of the estate in the mid-1980s make depressing reading:

> (the estate) . . . has traditionally had a high child population, an above average household size for the city, a higher level of unemployment and more unskilled and low-income households than the city as a whole (p1) . . . It has an above average level of social services support, low incomes and high fuel debts and rent arrears (p.2) . . . (it) is a severely deprived area. . . . Juvenile crime figures are relatively higher than in most other areas in Hull. The attendance at the estates' schools is the lowest in Humberside . . . Lack of employment opportunities and poor housing conditions have combined to produce a cycle of blight and social malaise, and given the estate a city-wide reputation as a 'sink estate', in low demand.

There was little doubt that the estate's stigma affected many of its residents. Some felt 'ashamed' to admit that they lived on the estate. Others were embarrassed to invite friends to their homes:

> I don't have people coming to visit me. There's nothing wrong with my flat but I don't want people coming down here to see me, I go out, because it's a trip. You can't even guarantee they'll be able to open the door when they get here. . . . It's embarrassing actually to say this is where I live. It's that bad'. Young people who lived on the estate and attended the local school adjacent to it were also affected 'If somebody asks yer what school you go to and you say [its name] they all turn their noses up, don't they? They all say 'down and outer. God what do yer go there for?' It's the area and people get a bad influence.

Neighbourliness

Nevertheless, despite the problems of both estates, Table 6 suggests quite a high level of neighbourliness amongst residents. It is on this basic bedrock of neighbourliness, perhaps, that most community crime prevention initiatives seek to build (see Chapter 2), hopefully converting a concern for immediate neighbours into concern for wider neighbourhood affairs. As one tenant on the London experimental estate commented 'In some ways it's quite a family estate . . . it just seems that most people know (one another) on the estate, if not to talk to, to nod to. I never get the feeling that there's a lot of bad feeling, there's not a lot of animosity.'

Table 6
Neighbourliness
(survey responses—1987) percentages

| | Hull | | London | |
	PEP	control	PEP	control
talk to, or are friendly with, two or more neighbours	51	60	52	67
friends with two or more households on estate	63	67	57	55
neighbours now keep watch on property when out . . .	62	69	66	55
. . . or would be happy for them to do so	33	24	27	39
BASE (respondents)	578	480	242	382

Summary

At the outset of the study, the two estates selected to become new PEPs both had high crime rates and adverse design and social characteristics. However, the Hull estate conformed more closely to the typical image of the problem estate on which PEP works—it was larger, poorer and seemed more disorderly and disorganised. Importantly, although the estates had comparable levels of more serious offences—burglary and motor crime particularly—the Hull estate had a greater level of disorderliness, associated with youth in particular, which fostered a greater sense of insecurity amongst residents, particularly women. Nevertheless, despite the difficulties of both estates a certain basic and low-level degree of neighbourliness seemed to survive—a potential which PEP might be able to develop.

4 Implementing PEP: the tenants' perspective

Although both experimental estates were exposed to the principal aspects of the PEP model, the approach adopted on each of the estates—both by PEP and the respective local authority—was rather different and this had a significant impact on the residential community. Glennerster and Turner's (1993) study (forthcoming) provides a detailed analysis of the implementation of all the various ingredients of the PEP model (see Chapter 1). This chapter concentrates on the ethnographic research into the implementation of PEP, especially concerning changes in the quality of the landlord-tenant relationship, an important precursor for the types of positive community development noted in Chapter 2.

The London experimental estate

PEP's work on the London experimental estate was part of an initiative to establish eight estate-based housing offices covering all the estates in a particular neighbourhood. The office on the experimental estate was the last to open, and in the first year of its existence was run by a housing manager who appeared to have little sympathy with the PEP approach. This caused friction between the manager and tenants and led to considerable conflict between the housing office and the PEP consultant. The housing manager was seen to be obstructive at meetings. Tenants complained that he failed to respond to their demands and instead of nurturing tenant involvement actually discouraged it. As one tenant put it:

> I think PEP could perhaps educate estate management into liaising with people . . . if they could perhaps educate them that we're trying to foster community relationships rather than destroy 'em and rather than try and get a 'them' and 'us' situation which it obviously is at the moment, they should be trying to say they (the tenants) are the customer and you should be working with them not against them.' Another tenants association member said: 'I just feel so frustrated. Week after week the same things come up and every single week you get the same assurances that something's going to be done . . . (the staff) have so little respect for the T.A. . . We're seen as a nuisance really.

When the research began in 1987, a tenants association had already been established on the estate and had made considerable progress. It prevented the tenants' hall being used as the site for the local office, succeeded in removing a child molester from the estate, exerted pressure on one particular family (responsible for much of the graffiti) who eventually moved out, and became quite vocal with the council about some of the problems which affected the estate, for example getting the lifts replaced and dealing with the cockroach infestation. Although the local office did not open until August 1987, a keen and enthusiastic PEP consultant worked with the tenants association in its infancy and provided practical support and assistance. Prior to the research, therefore, some improvement in the quality of housing service had already occurred. The second PEP consultant was responsible for getting the local office established, as well as working with caretakers and tenants on the estate. He set up a Tenant Forum where housing staff were asked to listen, explain and respond to tenants' grievances. This began the process of tenant consultation.

In the eleven month period between the formation of the tenants' association in November 1986 and October 1987 the morale of the tenants grew and they came to view PEP's presence as positive. The caretakers' attitudes also improved as a result of PEP's work, as did the condition of the estate (as measured by the regular environmental survey—Glennerster and Turner) and despite a number of reorganisations of repairs contractors, the rate of completed repairs also improved. In a matter of months the caretakers changed from being embittered frontline representatives of the council, of whom tenants were always critical, to people who identified with the tenants (believing it was in all their interests to live on a cleaner and more pleasant estate), and improved their performance. Two of the caretakers suggested ways in which the service they provided could be improved. Many of these changes had been brought about by the work the consultant had undertaken with the caretakers. Unfortunately, the housing manager proved unreceptive to the caretakers' ideas, did not encourage or pressurise them to maintain this new level of service and standards began to decline once more.

In June 1988 PEP withdrew from the estate because of the problems its staff were experiencing with the housing manager, but resumed work in October 1988 following the appointment of a new team leader. The effect of PEP's withdrawal was dramatic: the tenants' association was disbanded without the support of the consultant; the service from the local office, which was scarcely manned over the summer months, was practically non-existent; and the physical condition of the estate declined rapidly. The environmental survey (Glennerster and Turner) revealed that the estate which had scored 23 out of a possible 100 (for litter, graffiti and the like) in November 1987, reached 30/100 in January 1988, and a peak of 46/100 in the summer of 1988. As noted in Chapter 2, if vandalism goes unchecked, and the environment seems uncared for, abuse will become more prevalent because these visual signs of decay suggest that a neighbourhood is defeated and unable to contain or deter the delinquent element within it.

The sense of hope that PEP's presence on the estate had generated disintegrated with its withdrawal and tenants became demoralised—partly because they had not been consulted about PEP's withdrawal from the estate.

'We had hope with PEP on the estate' one tenant said 'that things will be getting done—now there's no hope.' By the time PEP resumed work, their consultants' workload in the neighbourhood as a whole had been significantly reduced. Two of the three PEP consultants working in the area were to be removed, leaving the remaining consultant alone to liaise with all the local offices including the experimental estate. In October 1988 a part-time tenant support worker was assigned to the experimental estate but, despite this assistance, in practical terms PEP's presence on the estate was nominal after October 1988.

The tenants association was reformed when the new team leader took post and some of its previous members remained on the Committee. The office-holders eventually resigned and another tenant group was established although some of the original tenants continued their membership. No training was offered to tenants—for example, in how to run meetings, or to establish working parties to discuss problems with repairs, maintenance etc.—and the Committee (with the exception of the Bengali members, see Chapter 5) had few clear objectives. In fact one of the new tenants' association members, at the end of the research aptly articulated what had been required all along: 'the TA is never going to be effective unless we learn how the council system operates . . . really we (the TA) are as stupid now as we were when we started last November (1989). . . . We need to know how things work, we need that help so we can then make our own decisions. We can do it ourselves once we know how the system works.'

The second team leader proved to be very effective in terms of housing management and, unlike her predecessor, appeared genuinely concerned about promoting tenant involvement. However, as the PEP consultant remarked at the time: 'I think (the tenants) have a detached role . . . it's quite interesting because I think that the team are very keen, so they will take a lead on a lot of issues and they will go ahead and develop those issues and they have no clear plan within that about when and why tenants should be involved in that . . . it's almost like you have got a team which is very keen to do it and almost their keenness excludes the tenants.'

One of the crucial ingredients in PEP's approach to difficult-to-let estates is tenant consultation. In its most basic form, this involves consulting tenants about physical improvements which might be made on their estate. The consultation process, however, is as much designed to promote cohesion as to learn from consultation. Tenants are usually approached through a number of small block meetings and asked to describe the problems on their estate and the ways in which they might be rectified. A 'package' of improvements is then drawn up for tenants' approval. On the London experimental estate, the improvements package (secured entry and lift replacement) was chosen by the council without any prior tenant consultation as these had been agreed centrally as part of the Borough's advanced leasing programme—a means of fund estate improvements with loans raised privately. Although the installation of new lifts was seen as a priority by the tenants, that of a security system was not.

While the nature of the improvements was predetermined (as the money had already been committed), PEP workers wished to consult tenants about the variety of different ways such schemes might be implemented. Due to the persistent problems with the first team leader, the PEP consultant and the Deputy District Housing Manager conducted two consultation meetings on the estate in March 1988 without the participation of the team leader. A total of fifty tenants attended these two meetings. Although the consultation meetings were minuted, and tenants were assured that their preferences for particular schemes would be incorporated in the improvements, several months later the lifts and security works were installed to a standard specification, with none of the tenants' preferences included and without further consultation. The newly installed lifts were vandalised shortly after they were installed in 1989 and the security system was not yet operational at the end of the study period in July 1990.

The Hull experimental estate

PEP's involvement on the estate began in 1987 but the local office did not open until September 1988. Whilst the London PEP experienced a considerable turnover of personnel and little continuity from PEP or the local office, the Hull PEP experienced a greater degree of stability. The Hull PEP also differed from the London PEP in that tenants were offered the possibility of an estate management board (EMB). This involved a partnership between tenants and the local authority where the day to day management of the estate would be the responsibility of an elected board of tenants (who were in the majority), council officers and specialist representatives (cf Zipfel 1988). The establishment of an EMB on the estate was agreed in principle by local councillors in December 1987. However, in October 1988 councillors decided to reject the estate management option and put forward their own proposals for a Neighbourhood Management Committee (NMC). The NMC, a sub-committee of the Housing Committee, has less power and independence than an EMB because recommendations from the NMC must be approved by councillors. Reluctantly tenants accepted this option, suggesting that councillors might in future consider a full EMB if the NMC was successful.

The issue of tenant management dominated PEP's work on the Hull experimental estate. Tenant consultation was extensive (one meeting per 77—100 households). Volunteers for a steering committee were drawn from the block meetings. Most areas of the estate were represented and intensive tenant training was undertaken. The steering group was replaced by the elected representatives of the Neighbourhood Management Committee in the Autumn of 1989 following elections. A tenant support worker was employed by PEP in the Spring of 1989 to work with tenants.

About £1.5m was allocated by Estates Action for planned maintenance to improve the weather resistance of the system-built houses. In addition, some £1.3m was allocated for environmental improvements, following tenant consultation. For the houses, this involved the addition of front gardens, fencing, and blocking-off walkways through areas of housing. In effect, the aim was to replace the 'Radburn' warren of pathways with more 'defensible space' under the surveillance of residents. Some of these are illustrated in Figure 2. Further, a closed-circuit television system was added to the existing phone entry systems in the blocks of flats, their surrounding areas were fenced and landscaped to bring them within the curtilage of the block, and ground floor communal areas were improved and enclosed—again, conforming to defensible space principles. All the work to the flats had been completed by the end of the study period but the DoE-sponsored Community Refurbishment Scheme workforce (CRS) who were responsible for the environmental improvements had only completed about half the area of houses. This partial implementation actually had quite profound effects on crime and community life on the estate which are described in Chapter 6. The security work to the flats and the CRS work were enacted with full tenant consultation. The local authority sent individual questionnaires to every householder outlining the options for improvements and asking them to state their preferences. Block meetings were held with tenants in the flats to discuss proposed improvements. This consultation exercise reached the majority of households on the estate.

Figure 2

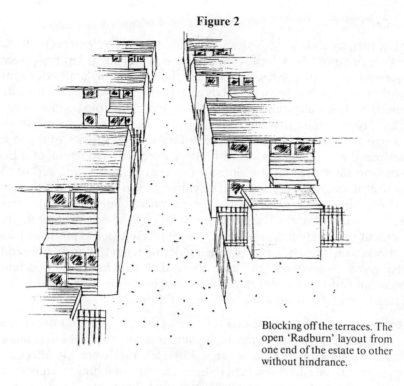

Blocking off the terraces. The open 'Radburn' layout from one end of the estate to other without hindrance.

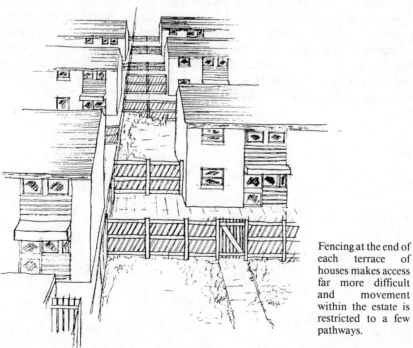

Fencing at the end of each terrace of houses makes access far more difficult and movement within the estate is restricted to a few pathways.

Conclusion

While Glennerster and Turner's study shows that the basic elements of PEP's housing service model—a local office, repairs, caretaking, lettings—were implemented on both estates, changes in the quality of landlord-tenant relationship—which has been the focus of this chapter—differed markedly between them. Ironically, the task of involving tenants on the London estate would have been much easier than on the Hull estate, given the pre-existence of an active tenants association, yet the unfortunate experience of the first housing team leader, combined with the subsequent reduction of PEP resources and the unilateral decisions of the local authority with regard to the physical improvements, served if anything to sap the morale of active tenants at a time when it could have been raised. Subsequent chapters suggest that, apart from the Bengali tenants, little in the way of community development occurred on the estate. In contrast, despite a less promising set of circumstances, the Hull PEP was a model of tenant consultation and responsiveness. Subsequent chapters show that this had an important influence on community development, though it was sorely tested by significant changes in the tenant population of the estate.

The experience of implementing PEP also shows that physical improvements to an estate and the quality of tenant consultation are of equal importance in community development on estates. Physical improvements affect all tenants, raise morale and give a firm indication that something is happening on an estate. They are the most visible sign that things are changing and, when tenants themselves have had a guiding hand in making those changes, inculcate a greater degree of interest and commitment. As one tenant commented: 'how can you ask them to come and join in the community and work for the good of the estate when they go back and see their doors and windows falling out? How much can you ask people to do without giving something back to them?'

5 Community change on the London PEP estate

Chapter 4 described the disappointment felt by the residents of the London PEP both with the inadequacies of the first housing team leader and with the effective withdrawal of PEP support. However, Table 7 shows that despite this set-back, 48 per cent of respondents in the second survey thought that the estate had improved over the past three years and the proportion of those satisfied with the estate increased from 52 per cent to 67 per cent. The trend in resident satisfaction was not, though, significantly greater than that which occurred on the control estate (see Chapter 7). Similarly, the rate of change in tenant turnover—i.e. the proportion of the population resident less than three years—was not significantly less than that of the control estate even though the proportion fell from 25 per cent to 22 per cent. As noted in Chapter 4, a tenants association had been established prior to PEP starting work and there was some expectation amongst the tenants that the estate would improve (34 per cent). Unfortunately, while expectations continued to rise on the control estate (see Chapter 7), the disappointments recounted in Chapter 4 would appear to have reduced expectations on the experimental estate (29 per cent versus 43 per cent on the control estate). However, there was a substantial reduction in the proportion of tenants on the experimental estate who said they would move if they had the chance (from 63 per cent to 49 per cent). All in all, the mixed feelings indicated by these results reflect the mixed experiences of the tenants during the study period.

Table 7
Changes in resident satisfaction and expectation—London estates percentages

	PEP estate		Control estate	
	pre	post	pre	post
satisfied with dwelling	56	62	64	67
satisfied with estate	52	67	54	62
estate improved over past 2/3 years	19	48	10	28
estate will improve over next 2 years	34	29	30	43
would move if had the chance	63	49	48	48
BASE (respondents)	242	268	382	393

The data was weighted by number of persons aged 16 years or over in a household. One interview was conducted per address, hence an individual's chance of selection depended upon the number of adults (aged 16+) resident at the selected household. Each respondent received a weight calculated by multiplying the number of people aged 16 or over at that address.

Nevertheless, despite these patchy results, the ethnographic research highlighted PEP's achievement in helping the Bengali tenants on the estate. The first survey found that about seven per cent of respondents ascribed Asian (Indian sub-continent) origin to themselves (Chapter 3, Table 1)—61 per cent of whom specifically described themselves as Bangladeshi. By the second survey, 17 per cent of respondents were of Asian origin. The increased number of Bengali tenants on the estate in large part reflected the housing policy of the local authority. Many of the Bengalis who moved onto the estate had little choice about their allocation of housing. From 1987, the Borough of Tower Hamlets' homeless families policy—of one offer of permanent accommodation only—effectively eliminated any tenant choice in an attempt to reduce the number of homeless families on the Borough's waiting list—predominantly Bengali—living in temporary bed and breakfast accommodation. At the outset, the neighbourhood in which the experimental estate was located was perceived by Bengalis to be a hostile and racist area devoid of any facilities suited to their needs, and at a distance from family and friends. Some of the first Bengali tenants who moved to the estate in the mid 1980s had experienced racial harassment.

In these circumstances the Bengalis might have been expected to be among the most disaffected people on the estate and the least likely to participate in activities. However, they actually benefitted substantially from PEP's presence and grew in confidence and strength during the life of the project. Their success can be attributed to a number of factors but the most important was that they were an identifiable minority group with a unified set of objectives—many originated from the Sylhetti region of Bangladesh and therefore had pre-existing cultural common links. The PEP consultant made direct contact with each of the Bengali households on the estate, facilitated the formation of a Bengali Association and negotiated access to the community clubroom so that daily Koran classes could be held for the children.

PEP's intervention facilitated communication between the Bengali residents and the housing office. In turn that communication helped to break down a number of misconceptions about the way in which the office, and the housing service in general, operated. As PEP's tenant development worker said, prior to their intervention:

> the Bengali group . . found communication lacking. They couldn't explain their problems to the local office and (it) seems that mistrust had arisen because their work (repairs etc) had not been carried (out) or it (took) longer . . so they were always wondering why the local office wasn't doing more for them . . . Once they knew that they could improve their lot by participation they took a very proper and higher role. (Before) they thought nothing's going to happen by joint association.

Once the Bengali Association was formed the consultant encouraged members to join the tenants' association. Such participation had a number of benefits. One of the leaders of the Bengali community observed:

PEP absolutely done (us) 100 per cent favour because myself and other people never bothered to go to TAs, anything like that, we didn't know there was a TA until PEP came around. . . . people . . . weren't scared to come to meetings because they (knew) there'll be someone there to (speak on their behalf). (Then) we had a communication between everyone living on the estate, between white people, black people, Indian, Bengali, whatever . . We had white neighbours but I'd never actually spoke to them. Through (the) TA we got to know them and they got to know us quite well. Better relations as result. Better neighbours.

The Bengali community was also able to draw on two active and effective leaders: firstly a young man in his 20s, and later, an older man with considerable involvement in Bengali affairs. Leadership is an important ingredient on those estates where tenant development and increased cohesion have occurred as a result of PEP's input (Rock, 1988). The young Bengali leader provided an important link between two very different cultures and was well respected by white and Bengali tenants alike. This young man was aware of the need to tread carefully with white tenants on the estate.

I was very diplomatic . . I . . don't go in there and . . say 'This is what I want for the Bengalis'. I don't go straight to the point, I go around, cover everyone (else's problems) then I get to the point. . . People respect you for it . . . people tend to think 'Oh he's alright' know what I mean, he cares about other people as well, not just for himself or his race.

PEP's work with the Bengalis on the estate may have long term benefits for both the Asian and the indigenous white population in terms of breaking down barriers and increasing understanding. PEP encouraged the Bengalis to participate and, three years later, white and Bengali tenants had equal representation on the tenants association committee. The Bengali leaders on the estate were also at the forefront of leadership in a neighbourhood-wide Bengali umbrella organisation also established with PEP's help. When asked to compare life on the estate three years ago with what it was like at the end of our research a Bengali tenant said: '100 per cent different . . I could go out near (the) estate anytime I want, . . it doesn't matter what time I'm going out, everyone knows me on the estate, I know who they are . . . In terms of the new families obviously it takes time for them to get used to the area but we actually encourage (them) by telling them what the situation is and (what it) was 3 or 4 years ago.' Active support networks also developed. Bengali tenants were welcomed by members of their community when they moved on to the estate and every assistance was given by the Bengali Association to help with any problems families might experience. As the tenant support worker noted: 'because the community (has) developed and some people have been there for quite a long time (and) settled down, among their own group there's a welcoming . . . (There's) somebody at hand and if they have a problem there is someone to help . . . they support each other . . . somehow or other

41

they settle down and feel quite comfortable.' In short PEP's intervention *empowered* the Bengali tenants. As a result they were able to deal with the problems which faced them because they were familiar with the appropriate structures and procedures. As one Bengali argued: 'To (this) day we still get harassment but they don't really take notice of it because they can handle it themselves now, they can come to the TA, complain about it, go to the estate office, etc. . . '

PEP's work may have also helped to reduce the resentment and bitterness of the younger generation of Bengalis. In areas like Spitalfields and Stepney, Asian youths have reacted strongly, and sometimes violently, to their experiences of harassment and prejudice. Fortunately, the young Bengalis on the estate did not exhibit the same degree of anger because their experiences of harassment had been less frequent and intense. The tenant development worker argued:

> The youth are very angry . . . about what has happened in schools, about what's happened in job prospects and everybody must help to redress that . . . The youths on (this estate) are very well behaved and (are not like) the youths in Spitalfields and Stepney. Their youth are very very angry, they are aggressive and they are fighting much harder. (On this estate) they haven't had much problem of open harassment, they haven't had (this thing) of knowing that so and so's kids been harassed, beaten up. This is balancing the children.

The local home beat officer suggested that on a neighbouring estate where race relations were poor it was the presence of 'antagonistic youths' which caused the problems, along with the behaviour of one or two families. These features did not appear to be present on the experimental estate. But despite the absence of conflict, and the relative contentment of many Bengalis on the estate, some—especially members of the older generation—and those who experienced a multitude of problems (particularly those relating to health) were not happy there and still wanted to be housed in the E1 area (Spitalfields, Whitechapel and Stepney). Nevertheless, the view of one of the Bengali spokesmen on the experimental estate is high praise indeed for PEP: '(this) is the best estate to live on at the moment in Tower Hamlets, in terms of race relations. I'm not talking about the housing. (That) is a general problem for everyone . . whoever you are, ethnic, white or black, everybody's facing the same problem . . but in terms of race relations (this estate) is the best place to live.'

Racially-motivated victimisation

On both the PEP and the control estates, neither the pre- nor the post-implementation survey found that households of Asian origin were more likely to be victimised than others. In fact, both Vietnamese and Asian households appeared significantly less victimised from household offences

42

than others. However, Asians were more likely than other groups to think that their victimisation was racially-motivated (Table A.1 in Appendix 3). Table A.2 also shows that Asians on the experimental estate, following PEP's activities, were significantly less likely than before to think that their victimisation was racially-motivated. A similar reduction on the control estate was not statistically significant, largely because victimisation in general declined considerably (see Chapter 7). Thus, while PEP's efforts were not sufficient to reduce the victimisation of Asian residents, it would appear that, for whatever reason, Asian victims no longer felt victimised on the estate by virtue of their ethnic identity.

Demoralisation

Ironically, while the Bengali tenants were 'empowered' over the three years of research, white and Afro-Caribbean residents became demoralised. They resented the dramatic rise in the number of Bengali families moving on to the estate and felt it no longer 'belonged' to them. While this experience might be dismissed as pure racism or simply a temporary problem in trying to adapt, it also represented perhaps a competition for symbolic territorial control. There is nothing unique in this situation as literature from both Britain and the United States reveals that as minority groups settle in previously white areas, a 'flight response' might result (Yancey & Erikson, 1979 see also Foster 1990). A similar response can also result where one ethnic group is succeeded by another (cf Taub *et al.*, 1984).

When the research began in 1987, there was already concern among many of the white tenants about the rise in the number of Bengali families—though at that time there were only some 15 Bengali households in the two large blocks out of a total of 214 households. Between autumn 1988 and spring 1989 a number of white tenants interviewed expressed a desire to buy their flats not only because it offered them some protection if the council sold the estate but also because the price of private housing was booming in the area. By September 1989, however, these same tenants no longer saw a future in remaining on the estate and expressed a wish to leave. This transition occurred because tenants became demoralised. The estate no longer seemed to belong to them and became a place where they felt increasingly uncomfortable. One woman told me: 'they're (Bengalis) just driving other people out you know. . . . They outnumber us in here now . . . I wouldn't like to move I love my flat (but) I feel I'm being pushed out . . . by who's coming in.'

In this climate, white residents became apathetic rather than aggressive. This occurred because, with the exception of the Bengalis, the tenants on the estate were a disparate group with little in common. They felt they could not prevent the changes which were occurring on the estate as the council made it clear that their priority was to house homeless families. While privately resenting the incoming Bengali households, the white tenants were faced with a

43

cohesive group who had common aims and interests, were supported by PEP and, as they gained confidence, became more forthright in making demands. As the Bengalis became a more cogent force, overt conflict became less likely because the Bengali community were perceived to be a powerful and articulate group. Yet when told how favourably many of the Bengalis felt towards the estate, one white woman tenant replied: '(I suppose it's) because we are tolerant of each other . . . in our back-handed sort of way . . . we do (think) they're here to stay, so that's it, end of story, so live and let live. Our resentment we keep more or less to ourselves, hence we become apathetic.'

The council's policy towards homeless families may in the long term prove to be misguided. In the first place, in the eyes of both Bengali and white tenants, it may do little to create balanced communities. The young Bengali leader felt integration was important but difficult to achieve if the council continued to pursue its policies: 'in five years time (the estate) will (be) full of Bangladeshis . . . it's growing every month, every week.' Second, the policy was very unpopular with Bengali tenants because they could not exercise any choice in the allocation of their housing. Although Bengali tenants wanted to move to estates where other Bengalis were housed they did not want to live on predominantly Bengali estates. One Bengali woman said: 'I prefer it where there are not too many Bengali families, just a few.' As noted in Table 7, when respondents were asked if they felt the estate would improve in the next two years there was a 5 per cent decrease, compared with a 13 per cent increase on the London control estate. It may be that this decrease reflects the feelings of tenants who fear that the continuing allocation of homeless families to the estate will be an undermining influence, setting in train another period of deterioration.

With hindsight, it would appear that PEP's work with the Bengali community should have been complemented by encouraging greater tenant involvement from other residents on the estate not only from the whites and Afro-Caribbeans, but from the Vietnamese and Chinese too (who were infrequently contacted and received little specific support from the PEP workers or the local office). The size of this latter group appeared to decline between the two surveys from 9 per cent to 4 per cent of the estate's population—though it is difficult to tell whether this was due to actual movement away from the estate or an increase in non-response to the survey from this ethnic group; either would be indicative of the 'withdrawal' of this minority group from the estate.

Demographic changes on the experimental and control estates

Table 8 illustrates two important and divergent trends in the demographic compositions of the two London estates over the study period. In the first place, there was a relatively greater increase in the elderly, in single-person households and unemployed people on the experimental estate. By the end of the study period, there were substantially more people in these categories than on the control estate. Although the survey showed the proportion of households receiving housing benefit declined by 37 per cent, this compared with a 54 per cent reduction on the control estate. Thus, by the end of the study period, the experimental estate had become more elderly and financially-dependent than the community on the control estate. Interestingly, the proportion of households in owner occupation remained low on the experimental estate (6 per cent) but increased from 4 per cent to 14 per cent on the control estate, reflecting perhaps both a growth in income and confidence amongst some at least on the control estate.

Second, Table 8 shows that while both estates saw an increase in their ethnic minority populations, the size of the Asian, primarily Bengali, population on the control estate rose to almost the level of the white population. Thus, in a very literal sense, the Asian/Bengali group was no longer a 'minority' on the estate. As will be seen in Chapter 7, these two demographic trends may have brought about a greater social stability and cohesiveness on the control estate which did not occur amongst the more disparate and poorer population on the experimental estate.

Table 8
Demographic changes on the London estate—household surveys
percentages

	experimental estate		control estate	
	pre	*post*	*pre*	*post*
resident less than 3 years	24	24	17	23
persons over 60 yrs	23	29	25	18
households with 1 adult only	38	46	34	36
adults (16yrs+) not in full-time employment	67	73	63	66
owner occupiers	6	6	4	14
receiving housing benefit	27	17	26	12
Social Classes A-C2	28	30	31	29
Social Class D	24	23	26	38
Social Class E	47	47	43	33
Asian	7	17	30	41
Black	10	16	6	6
White	73	58	57	44
BASE (respondents)	242	268	382	393

responses weighted by number of adults in household.

Summary

At the end of the study period, residents' feelings about the London experimental estate were mixed, reflecting the mixed experiences of the past three years. PEP did bring about a greater sense of security and a real increase in the Bengali residents' feelings of safety from racially-motivated victimisation. This was achieved not only through *enablement*—that is, providing them with facilities and meeting their demands so that they felt they had become capable of achieving something—but also through *empowerment*—that is, helping them to achieve a more powerful position on the estate. Though, in fact, the Bengalis were no more likely to be singled-out for victimisation than other households on the estate, either before or after PEP's involvement, it would seem that they were helped, thanks to PEP's efforts, to actually believe that they were facing a risk equal to other groups and that they were not being victimised by virtue of their ethnicity alone.

Nevertheless, despite the better prospects for the Bengali residents, the other residents on the London experimental estate had become poorer and more heterogeneous, at least in comparison with the London control estate. As will become apparent in Chapter 7, these demographic trends, coupled with the sense of demoralisation which neither the actions of PEP nor the council were able to dispel, were insufficient to bring about significant changes in crime and community life on the experimental estate, in contrast to the control estate where conditions did in fact improve considerably.

6 Community change on the Hull PEP estate

This Chapter describes the way in which the residential community changed on the Hull experimental estate during the study period. It describes the culture of the estate community as it related to crime at the outset of the study and subsequently how this altered as a result of changes in environmental design, housing service, tenant organisation and tenant allocations.

The estate cultures

A characteristic of 'problem' estates is a high rate of population turnover. Not surprisingly, in the survey taken at the beginning of the study period, 38 per cent of adults (aged 16 years and over) on the experimental estate had been resident for less than four years (the figure was 26 per cent for the control estate). However, 41 per cent had lived there for more than 13 years (as on the control estate). This suggests the existence of two groups, a transient population which turns over relatively frequently and a stable population which has remained on the estate for several years. The ethnographic research confirmed that the Hull experimental estate was divided into these separate groups. There were established tenants, some of whom had lived on the estate since it was built. This group tended to be stable and, although many of its members were unemployed, they seemed to 'make ends meet' on meagre incomes. Such tenants were more likely to be involved in community activities available on and around the estate, exercised supervision (often strict) over their children and had little experience of crime and offending (except as victims). They were also in the forefront of tenant activity and many were determined to reverse the estate's decline.

Members of the second group were a more diverse collection of tenants. In general, they seemed altogether more 'vulnerable' and less able to cope with various economic and social vicissitudes. Within this loose collection, there were a number of 'problem' families who tended to have graver and more numerous social and financial problems, and more persistent contact with law enforcement, social services and other official agencies. Similar differences in lifestyle, values and outlook have been found in many past and present studies of community life on problem housing estates (see Reynolds, 1986 for a review; see also Bottoms et al., 1989).

Contact between the various 'vulnerable' groups of tenants and the established tenants was minimal. Interactions within the vulnerable group, including contact with the 'problem' tenants, were more frequent and in some respects it was only possible to distinguish 'problem' from other vulnerable tenants by the degree rather than the type of problems they experienced. An exploitative and self-perpetuating subculture had developed in which some vulnerable tenants found themselves locked in a cycle of deprivation in circumstances which they perceived to be out of their control. Many found it impossible to cope financially. 'Family life' often lacked stability and was marked by tension and sometimes physical violence.

All tenants were affected by the criminal activity which occured on the estate, though the 'established' tenants appeared more insulated from it than others. They had more control over their lives generally, tended not to mix with the vulnerable tenants and often took precautions to prevent theft. Their methods did not necessarily rely on physical crime prevention, for example they might simply involve 'keeping an eye' on each others properties. In many cases the 'problem' and other vulnerable families found it difficult to trust one another so that informal crime prevention was undermined. Some of those who were heavily involved in crime on the estate prided themselves on the fact that their reputation hindered them from being victimised themselves. However there were many vulnerable tenants, particularly single parents, who suffered from repeat victimisations. One eighteen year old woman, with two young children and a boyfriend recently released from prison, during her eighteen months on the estate had experienced one actual and one attempted break-in, had dog excrement put through her letter box, and had her windows smashed on several occasions.

'Problem' families

There were about a dozen families with whom the local office had regular contact and who caused problems on the estate. 'There's a few bad families' a tenant remarked, 'I think 90 per cent of people would like to get rid of the other 10 per cent'. However, there was one particular family who were regarded by tenants and housing staff alike as responsible for the majority of the problems. Most of these problems emanated from their children who were clearly beyond parental control. They often roamed the estate until the early hours of the morning and, with other children who were attracted to their group, stole, vandalised, rode motorcycles, threatened and terrorised tenants. One of the residents said:

> There's only certain areas (of the estate) where they are (where they live) but with the estate being open they can get from one side of the estate to the other and disrupt the whole estate . . . . it's motorbikes. If you've got a moped or a motorbike, you have to have it locked up or they'll swipe it . . . even yer sheds aren't safe 'cos if they know there's a motorbike in the shed they'll break in and get the motorbike, steal it, strip it down and use it for riding around . . . There are a group of these people who do it. They're all lads between eight and 18 . . . eight year olds riding on mopeds—they can't even reach the pedals.

The local caretaker continued in the same vein:

> It's the same gang (who cause the trouble) . . . there's some gypsies (sic)
> that . . . (have) been a problem for a hell of a long time . . . if you ask
> . . . everybody in this block or the people around the block, who the
> majority of damage is done by they say the (name of family) . . . because
> they're always involved . . .

Although this family were stigmatised by tenants and provided a convenient
scapegoat for the estate's problems—as much because they were gypsies as
the trouble they caused—they were certainly responsible for a number of the
incidents which took place on the estate. As the housing manager argued:
'Our friends' . . . are accused of everything. I don't think they are involved
in everything . . . They are an easy scapegoat, although without a doubt they
are at the centre of a lot of problems (especially) vandalism.'

Fifty-six teenagers who lived on the estate and attended the local
comprehensive school completed a questionnaire similar to that
administered to residents. Seventy-six per cent of these young people regarded
disturbances by youths and teenagers to be 'a big problem' (39 per cent) or
'something of a problem' (37 per cent). Many of them mentioned this
particular family by name. Given that one might expect teenagers to be more
sympathetic to their peers, their comments about the problems on the estate
and those who caused them were suprisingly condemnatory: 'the estate is a
bit of a dump with kids hanging around in large groups at night. Smashing
up people's houses and threatening people, glass being thrown, abuse to old
people, dogs . . .' Another said: 'the estate is full of kids who mess about and
vandalise the area'. Forty-four per cent of respondents in the 1990 survey
believed that disturbances from youths and teenagers were a 'big problem'
on the estate, a figure which was almost double that of any of the other estates
included in the research.

Reynolds (1986), in her study of a 'problem estate', highlighted the impact
that a tiny proportion of young people can have on a housing estate. She
argued that although a particular group of troublemakers 'constituted only
one per cent of the teenage population . . . there was a sense in which the
estate belonged to them more than anyone else'. Others have argued that a
concentration of families with a lax parental discipline 'will produce a more
than proportional increase in vandalism and delinquency' (Wilson 1980:47).
The comments of one young person interviewed sum up the way adolescents
in a poor environment get drawn into trouble: 'When you first move up here
(on to the estate) you think it's, you know, really really rough. But if you've
lived here for a couple of years or something like that you get used to the
people and what they're like. You think well I moved here and you could say
I was the odd one out but live there a couple of years and you get to like
them. They just take you as you are.'

49

Many parents feared for their children growing up in such an environment. As one single parent said: 'You daren't do anything because of what they might do to yer bairns or yer home. I can look after meself but the bairns just drift along with the rest of 'em'. The headmaster of the comprehensive school located next to the estate argued that the influence which the most troublesome family and their children had on the estate and on the other young students in the school was considerable. He suggested that these children had encouraged others to play truant and to become involved in more serious criminal activities. Most of the parents of these children seemed to absolve themselves of any responsibility for their offspring's activities and, for some, just getting through the daily business of living was a major task. Some of the parents of these troublesome youths were heavily involved in crime themselves and the most prominent 'problem' family had a highly developed and cohesive network of other family and friends on the estate. Their network was not dissimilar to that which Polii Xanthos (1989:75/9) described on 'Gardenia' in Sheffield, except that the family had only lived on the estate for a very short period of time (3/4 years).

Vulnerable families

There were a significant number of single parents—mostly women—on the estate, many of whom were very young. They often seemed alienated and suffered most from the destabilising impact of the estate's 'subterranean' culture. They received intermittent support from boyfriends or husbands whose lifestyles often brought them into contact with the police and, eventually, prison. In the local prison, where their men tended to be remanded, further criminal contacts developed which were sometimes reinforced by extensive kinship networks back on the estate. There was a desperation among many of the women about their lives. Few thought beyond the present and many wanted to leave the estate.

For the other vulnerable families, the estate was an environment which was both seductive, because there were many other people like them who shared their attitudes, values and problems, and destabilising, because the presence of other such families made it more difficult for them to break with the old. The subculture on the estate offered members of these families, particularly the men, a network of contacts where there were opportunities to steal and networks to sell stolen goods. One of the tenants described it thus:

> you can buy anything in these pubs (on the estate) anything you want from a rabbit to a video, . . . alarm clocks, anything . . . I've never seen anything like it. I've been in there and they've walked in . . . with two carrier bags of alarm clocks £1 a piece and they've gone like that . . . people walk in to (the supermarket) and walk out with something 'cos they know how the camera works, they know—oh it's gonna be 15 seconds, then it's gonna go over there . . . and the devils walk in and

buy something and they watch these cameras and they'll see and they'll do it a few times. I know, I've seen them walking round doing it, just looking, they don't have to steal anything at the time they just work out the system. And then what happens you get to a phase where the thing on the market is Maxwell House (coffee), boxes and boxes of Maxwell House. Why?—because the camera's taking maybe 60 (seconds) or more to get back to the Maxwell House. Then you go into (the supermarket) again and you find the Maxwell House is being changed and it's now tomato sauce, and then that's the next thing on the market.

There was also persistent shoplifting of clothes in the major department stores of the city centre and more organised activity:

> tobacco is one of the biggest things, there's a lot of tobacco gets through the Docks, and it's obvious(ly) through the back way you know, and then you can buy tobacco at £2.50 a belt, it's saving about £1.50 . . . it comes in large quantities. There's a lot of it on this estate. I've never known an estate like this one in my life . . . (there are a) large amount of crooks.

The effect of living on an estate with an established subterranean culture was that the younger generation, both teenagers growing up on the estate and the young people being housed there, fed into the groups which sustained it. Among families where there were many problems, even very young children were left to play unsupervised on the estate for hours at a time. One evening one of the researchers witnessed a toddler, seemingly no more than three years old, climbing over a seven foot fence onto to the top of the porch of his home and thence climbing through the fan light of a bedroom window. Inevitably these children's view of the estate was one where they could do as they pleased because few attempted to stop them (cf. Morgan, 1978).

Changes on the estate

During the study period three kinds of changes occurred on the experimental estate:

    i. environmental design modifications (Estates Action)
    ii. management changes and tenant involvement (PEP)
    iii. tenant allocations.

Environmental design modifications

As described in Chapter 4, there were extensive planned maintenance, security and defensible space improvements to the blocks of flats and also defensible space improvements to the houses. By the end of the study period, only about a third of the houses had received the defensible space modifications and the estate could be divided physically into five areas, illustrated in Figure 1. *Area A* consisted of the improved area of houses, with

51

defensible space modifications. *Area B* consisted of those houses which had not yet benefited from the improvement programme. *Area C* consisted of a group of three of the tower blocks. *Area D* comprised the other tower block, physically separate from *Area C,* and *Area E* comprised the three smaller blocks of flats.

Management changes and tenant involvement

The effort of PEP on the experimental estate was in many respects a model of tenant involvement. Those who were involved in the Neighbourhood Management Committee and the Community Association felt that a community feeling was developing on the estate and, despite the problems caused by a minority, felt optimistic about the future. One tenant commented 'the whole attitude of the way the tenants are thinking is slowly changing'.

Tenant allocations

There were however significant changes in the social mix on the estate over the study period. The proportion of residents who had lived on the experimental estate for less than three years increased from 26 per cent to 28 per cent, while the proportion declined on the control estate from 19 per cent to 16 per cent (t=+2.180, p.<.05). Though the proportion of households receiving housing benefit declined on both estates, the rate of decline on the experimental estate—from 39 per cent to 34 per cent—was significantly less than on the control estate—from 35 per cent to 22 per cent (t=+3,276, p.<.01). These changes were accompanied by changes in household composition—fewer respondents were married or cohabiting (t=−1.944, p.<.05), fewer were adult-only households (t−2.6505, p<.01) and there were fewer adults per household (t=−3.0345, p.<.01). These changes were due to the different characteristics of newcomers to the estate. Compared with recent tenants in the earlier (1987) survey, newcomers in the later (1990) survey were less likely to be married or cohabiting (d.f. 535, t=−2.344, p<.05) and more likely to be in receipt of housing benefit (d.f. 535, t=+3.209, p.<.01). Thus notwithstanding the improvements brought about under the auspices of PEP, the social position of the estate worsened relative to the control estate. However, the effect was by no means uniform, with significant consequences for community life in different parts of the estate.

Differential tenant allocation

The changes in tenant turnover interacted with the design changes to produce by the end of the study period different social mixes in the different parts of the estate. These are summarised in Table 9. Prior to the design changes, the two areas of houses (Areas A and B) offered similar accommodation and had roughly similar social compositions. However, turnover in the improved area of houses (Area A) declined significantly (t=−3.2884, p.<.01) (for method see Appendix 1). The design improvements seemed to have altered the relative

Figure 3. The Estate

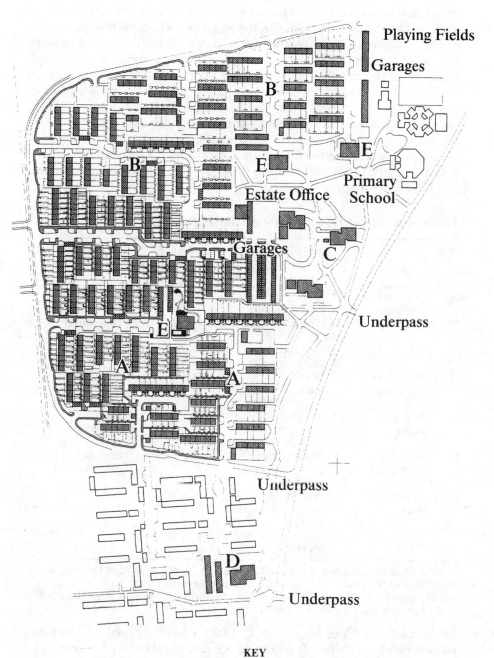

Playing Fields

Garages

B

E

B

E

Estate Office

Primary School

Garages

C

Underpass

E

A

A

Underpass

D

Underpass

KEY

A: improved area of houses
B: unimproved area of houses
E: the smaller blocks
C: the three tower blocks
D: the single tower block

53

desirability of the estate for tenants in this part of the estate—here, the proportion of residents who were satisfied with their homes increased from 65 per cent to 91 per cent and with the estate as a whole from 46 per cent to 67 per cent. Because more tenants stayed, in contrast to the general trend on the estate, the residents in Area A as a whole became relatively less poor—fewer households had members not in full-time employment (t=−2.874, p.<.05) and fewer were headed by people on very low incomes (t=−5.084, p.<.01). Though relative net turnover in the unimproved area of houses (Area B) did not increase significantly, its residential population became relatively more disadvantaged since the estate was receiving poorer households. More households were in receipt of housing benefit (t=+3.1041, p.<.01), and there were fewer adults (t=−3.0494, p.<.01) and more children (t=+2.8385, p.<.01) per household.

Table 9
The physical and social partitioning of the Hull PEP estate

Area	Description	Physical changes	Rate of tenant turnover[1]	change in social mix[2]
A.	improved area of houses	* environmental improvements (defensible space) * planned maintenance * anti-condensation	declined	* less poor * more couple-led households
B.	unimproved area of houses	* planned maintenance * anti-condensation	stable	* poorer * more households with children
C.	three tower blocks	* entry system * communal areas * landscaping	increased	* poorer * young * single
D.	the single tower block	* entry system * communal areas * landscaping	increased	* less poor * more females
E.	the smaller blocks	* entry system * communal areas * landscaping * sheltered scheme for elderly (2)	stable	* older * more females

[1]Turnover estimated from the household surveys by the relative net change in the proportion of respondents living on the estate for less than three years.
[2]Relative net change in social indicators derived from household surveys with a model of the form y = wave + treat + wave.treat.

In the past, the three tower blocks (Area C) had housed a substantial proportion of elderly people (about 42 per cent of residents). However, as a consequence of natural change, and a deliberate policy of concentrating older persons into the smaller blocks on the estate (Area E, two of which became sheltered housing), a greater number of vacancies arose in Area C and turnover increased rapidly (t = +4.8234, p. <.01). By the second survey (three years later), 44 per cent of Area C's population had been on the estate less than three years and 42 per cent of adults were aged 16—30 years (t = +2.7865, p. <.01). Vacancies in the Area C blocks were filled with non-family households, many in receipt of housing benefit (t = +3.001, p. <.01), especially formerly homeless, young single people and some recently released from youth custody or institutional care. To some extent, the concentration of the young singles in the Area C tower blocks came about as a consequence of high vacancies, limited suitability and low demand but there may have been also an element of selectivity since the relatively increasing vacancies in the other tower block—Area D (t = +2.5904, p. <.01) were not filled by the single homeless.

Positive developments

In general, PEP helped both established tenants and some of the new arrivals to assert a certain degree of control over their residential environments. Those who worked closely with PEP were genuinely committed to improving the estate and curbing the 'criminal element'. They resented the negative reputation of the estate and saw the key to its future in raising demand, pressurising those families who failed to conform and evicting 'problem' tenants: 'there are three families on this estate that I know in this area alone that if they were evicted from their properties people would cheer. It's not a nice thing to do to evict someone but I am thinking of the people of that area that live around (them). The settled people who were there before these people came along, they have rights surely.' Others said: '. . . the whole attitude of the way the tenants are thinking is slowly changing' .. '(we want to) raise the estate a lot more so instead of it being, 'oh well it's the (experimental estate) for you pal' it'll be 'can I get (a house on) the (experimental estate)? That's what we're aiming for is a place where people want to be, not have to be.'

The physical improvements were the most visible and frequently cited cause for enthusiasm. One tenant felt: 'they rekindled the spirit of the people . . . When they get their new front fences up their attitudes have begun to change. . . . this attitude (had developed) . . . that people just didn't care and there is a lot of people now . . . I mean, you go t'shops and they talk to yer and say 'Ooh, in'it nice now we've got our fronts . . . the attitude of the people's definitely got better. The way the tenants are using the (NMC) representatives to me shows that they believe something better is going to come along otherwise they wouldn't bother to come to us for help.'

Just over half the 56 teenagers who completed the questionnaire at the local school felt that the estate had improved in the last year. They wrote: '(the) houses have been painted, gardens made big and new fences put up.' 'it's more private and tidy'. Table 10 shows changes in tenant satisfaction recorded by the household surveys. The results were mixed: the improvements in satisfaction with the dwelling, including reductions in problems of dampness and exterior decor (the two main elements of the refurbishment scheme) were to some extent offset by similar reactions to dwelling improvements which had been carried out on the control estate. Neither, on the whole, had the level of tenant satisfaction changed (the multivariate analysis found an insignificant relative change) nor the desire of residents wanting to move from the estate. Nevertheless, there was an appreciable jump (from three per cent to 27 per cent) in the proportion of those who thought the estate had improved over the past two to three years and, encouragingly, a considerable increase in expectations of continuing improvements. As will become apparent, these mixed feelings reflect the mixture of positive and negative developments which had occurred on the estate.

Table 10
Changes in tenant satisfaction and expectation—Hull estates percentages

	PEP estate		Control estate	
	pre	post	pre	post
satisfied with dwelling	74	82	75	83
dampness in dwelling (a big problem)	39	28	41	28
exterior decor of dwelling (a big problem)	21	6	16	5
satisfied with estate	45	53	63	65
estate improved over past 2/3 years	3	27	6	13
estate will improve over next two years	19	47	12	10
would move if had the chance	53	51	42	46
BASE (respondents)	578	573	480	499

Data weighted by number of persons 16 years or over in household.

While it is understandable that tenants in the improved houses felt some optimism, it is more surprising that flat dwellers, despite many of the older tenants being as one put it almost 'at breaking point' (because of the problems caused by young people—see below) also expressed optimism. One woman told me: 'I feel certain that when things are complete and the builders have moved away it will be great.'

Many tenants who were involved in activities on the estate, particularly representatives of the Neighbourhood Management Committee, developed a sense of ownership about the estate. One of the resident representatives, when asked in what ways he felt PEP had improved things, replied:

> I think PEP have brought the people together . . . that's what happening now, your neighbours are taking more notice of their neighbours, . . . like if my garden was rubbish and my neighbour's was gorgeous they would say I'll report that and they'll go in the office and report it . . .

56

that's PEP. They're making people think oh this is nice I think we'll keep it like this . . . but they still need to be taught some of 'em . . . It's making them aware of what they've got now. If you think about it, the houses were really run down, they're making them look better so consequently the people inside feel better. I think it works that way . . . It gives you something to aim for, something to say 'I'm gonna look after this, this is ours . . . I like this estate . . . I wouldn't want to be anywhere else' . . . I think if more people started thinking the same way as I do we'd live in a better environment. This is our estate. I can nearly say this is my estate, now being on the NMC. I think its time people started pulling their socks up and thinking 'this is ours, let's make sure it stays ours, let's look after it as ours and not let people pull it down'.

This tenant also pointed to the importance of responsibility. He said that as a younger man he had never bothered with appearances: 'I was just the same as some other people. Maybe people looked over my garden and said, 'the lazy devil, why don't he get it dug' but now it's different. I've got the responsibility—I'm a part owner, if you like, of the estate and what the estate reflects, reflects me. If we're going to make this estate somewhere better to live then surely we must become better tenants or residents ourselves because we have to be an example for other people to follow.'

When asked what might have happened if PEP had not intervened one tenant said: 'It would be even worse now. It would definitely be worse. See, the thing is, once it's all finished and the trees are growing and everything's spick and span people'll turn round and say 'it's not a bad place to live after all.' I think that's the way it'll go and they're saying now 'it's just problem families you know, if we could just sort them out then the estate'd be brilliant' . . . I think it's got to a level where it's a 100 per cent better than it was . . . it must still improve further. I mean the main problem is vandalism . . . coming from 10 and 9 and 8 year olds.'

In the last few months of the study some tenants ran a tea-time club on the estate for young children. This generated a great deal of interest from the children on the estate. As one of the NMC representatives said: 'Even the kids are beginning to ask about things. Last week there was two 10 year olds and they said, ". . . are you gonna do anything on a Saturday?" So I said "Why?". They said "Well we get fed up on a Saturday there's nothing to do". For two ten years to say 'are you gonna do something' actually ask themselves 'are you gonna do something' cos there's nowt else to do on the estate . . . there's nowhere to go unless it involves travelling and expense like going to the leisure centres but people round here just haven't got the money, Janet. There's that much unemployment that they can't afford to send their kids to them places.'

The young and single

Due to a general shortage of council housing, neither of the London estates had a significant group of teenage single people living in their own flats. On

57

the Hull experimental estate in recent years practically all the flats in the three high rise blocks (Area C—Figure 1) were allocated to single homeless people. Many of these people were under 20. The teenagers found themselves homeless for a number of reasons: some had come out of local authority care, others had been released from youth custody, prison, or psychiatric institutions. The vast majority had left their parental home because of various stresses within the family and, because they had no fixed abode, became eligible for council housing.

Without information on the tenant allocation process across the entire local authority it is difficult to determine quite how the concentration of young people in these tower blocks came about. The unpopularity of the estate as a whole, combined with a policy of not allocating children to tower block flats, meant that the dwellings were in low demand and that tenants required few housing priority 'points' to become eligible for these dwellings. A need to fill vacant properties quickly—as recommended by PEP—made it relatively easy for homeless young people to qualify. The local authority also operated a Single Persons' Support Unit, one of whose functions was to find housing for those who were homeless after leaving their families or institutional care. It seemed that the unit adopted the (reasonable) approach of referring clients to the estates for which they expressed a preference from amongst those for which they were eligible for immediate accommodation. Possibly, the 'lively' reputation of the experimental estate amongst young people influenced their choice from amongst the few estates which had vacancies available to them.

Many of the teenagers who were housed on the estate were simply unable to adapt to running their own flat on very limited resources. Most of them were not working and survived on benefit payments. Youngsters often moved in without any furniture at all and there was a lucrative black market dealing in cookers, fridges and other household items. Given their meagre incomes, many of the young people quickly got into debt. The youngsters' problems were not restricted to finance. Placed in an environment where there was little informal social control or intensive support, some fell into 'bad habits and bad company'. This situation caused difficulties for the young people themselves and for other tenants on the estate who complained about the noise and nuisance, the destruction of council property, filthy and graffiti covered public areas, the anti-social hours which some young people kept and the deviant activities in which they were engaged.

The flats which were occupied by young tenants became magnets for other teenagers. As the caretaker explained: 'Of course, these young kids who's in here, I guarantee yer anybody under 20 living in one of these flats isn't working. Unfortunately, I'm not saying all young kids are bad, they're not, but it's out of that element that you get all the bother, not just with them but the people who come to visit 'em. We had a kid move into [a particular flat]. The first day up there, there were 13 people laid on his landing just waiting for him to come home. This is what you're up against. There's too many of 'em it's physically impossible to shift them all. . . . you're out numbered.'

58

One flat in the tower blocks became a haven for truants, runaways and other disaffected youngsters. Up to fifteen or sixteen teenagers congregated regularly in the flat during 1989. In many instances these 'hangers on' were unwelcome but once young tenants had got in with a 'bad crowd', they found it difficult to dissociate themselves. As the housing manager argued:

> If you'd have seen the 12th floor of [one of the blocks] you'd have been horrified. I went round with the surveyor and in a sort of cursory 10 minutes we reckoned there was £5,000 of damage just to the communal areas. It was a situation that got out of control. Basically that lad lost control of that flat at an early stage . . . basically that lad shouldn't have been given a flat. He wasn't ready for independent living. He has a history of petty crime and solvent abuse and he knew all the wrong people and they all came round to (his) flat cos it was like oh (he's) got a flat, open house, let's party . . . When the pressure was put on him to get rid of 'em he couldn't do it. I couldn't get rid of 20 people if they suddenly walked into my house. People sponged off him and that's what happened at other flats. They got their mates in and they suddenly lost control. Kids were coming in who should have been in school, girls of 13 and 14.

This was clearly a very difficult environment for young people especially as many were vulnerable because of their past experiences. No social controls existed once young people were allocated flats on the estate, except for the threat of eviction. By the time court orders were sought, the damage was already done. This was most clearly demonstrated by a fire which occurred in the flat of a teenage tenant. It was deliberately set alight by one of his 'friends'. The entire block of flats was evacuated in the early hours of the morning and extensive damage occurred to the flat itself—£37,000 worth of damage—and those surrounding it. In other cases teenagers demolished the internal walls of flats, smashed fixtures and fittings and so on.

The established tenants rarely sympathised with teenagers who were allocated flats and their feelings are not difficult to understand given the disturbances which some of these young people caused. One tenant's comments expressed the feelings of many: 'I felt I wanted to dig my heels in (and stay) . . . because we love this flat we really do love it and we don't want to move and the only reason that we are thinking of moving is for the conditions that we're having to put up with.' He said 'I won't have any of my friends down here now, how can you invite somebody. When they come in there's graffiti everywhere and the lifts are full of urine, you just can't.'

In October 1989 the local office received a deputation from some of the flat dwellers complaining 'about the type of people you're putting in the flats'. The housing manager on the estate admitted that many of the youngsters were 'feckless', ill-equipped for living alone, and had little consideration for their neighbours. It was his argument that changes in benefit payments to young people had contributed to the problems which the housing office faced: 'the benefit changes were forcing more people out of dependent accommodation. It was penalising people for having non-dependents at home but those people weren't able to live independently . . . it started to manifest itself with the kind of people we were picking up. We had this big pool to choose from to go into the flats and as that pool increased and the points level depressed sooner or later we were bound to hit people who were bad'uns . . . so all the pressures came together and gradually into 1989 . . . people started congregating at certain flats and we made two or three bad allocations.'

Although many of the young tenants experienced considerable problems adapting to life on the estate in a conventional sense, it would be quite misleading to suggest that their experience of living on the estate was an alienating and isolating one. In fact the most worrying aspect of the widespread allocation of flats to young people on the experimental estate was the speed with which a youth subculture developed. Ironically while the established tenants were doing their best to force housing management to rethink their allocation policies so that the young homeless were not housed on the estate, young people were requesting flats on the experimental estate because they perceived it to be a lively place, full of opportunity and contacts for young people to have 'a good time'. Unfortunately, many of these opportunities and contacts were directly concerned with a criminal subculture. As a housing manager argued: '. . . the younger people, they seem to mingle in more . . . they all know each other. It's just amazing really, they all know each other. There's like a network of young lads.' This network was comprised not only of young people who lived on the estate but those from other areas who had friends on the estate 'a lot of trouble (in the tower blocks) was caused by people coming in . . . it used to draw people in (partly because of the school). (The school) might be tucked away on the top right hand corner of the estate but it still has a lot of connections with the rest of the area.' This view was supported by the home beat officer too.

Much of the aimlessness and disaffection prevalent among young people on the estate was associated with unemployment. There was a considerable number of young people between the ages of 17 and 28 who had never worked. A local youth worker in the area described them as 'hopeless cases'. With no jobs and no hope some teenagers turned to drugs, an activity which was facilitated by the subterranean culture. Drug abuse created an instability of its own which, unless curbed, was likely to result in a further increase in crime and other social problems. Fifty-one per cent of the teenagers from the experimental estate who completed the questionnaire felt drug abuse was a 'big problem' (41 per cent) or 'something of a problem' (10 per cent). Eighteen per cent of respondents in the first (1987) survey felt that 'people using illegal drugs' was a 'big problem', a figure which had doubled by the second (1990) survey. It is perhaps a reflection of the levels of deprivation on the estate that some of this drug abuse involved injecting prescribed drugs (obtained from GP's on prescription and subsequently sold on) rather than the use of heroin or cocaine.

Out of care

Flats were also allocated to older single people with a history of alcohol abuse and mental illness. The proportion of residents who thought that people hanging around drinking on the estate was a big problem increased from 25 per cent in the first (1987) survey to 43 per cent in the second (1990). The young people interviewed were also sensitised to 'drunks hanging around the shops'. The drunks were often abusive to shoppers and in some cases were a danger to themselves. As one of the caretakers said 'there's this chappie, half past one in the morning he's laid on his doorstep with a cider bottle in his hand. I got a telephone call to say he was there. So I said to the woman (tenant) 'What's he doing?', 'He's laying on the doorstep with a cider bottle in his hand and there's a gas canister in the doorway with the top off. He's 60 odd but they do it, don't they, when they can't get the booze and what not.'

One alcoholic visited during the research in the company of a probation officer was an agoraphobic. He received his benefit cheque every Thursday and saved 80p from his previous week's money so that he could have a drink before facing the trip to the post office. Once he had collected his cheque he drank until the money was gone (usually by the weekend) and was imprisoned in his flat for the rest of the week. There were also a small number of people resident on the estate who had a history of sex-offending. Clearly this was a concern to many residents: 'There's so many queer people walking about. We've had people in the flats. Someone used to ring this phone box here when not just girls but young boys as well (passed by). Children are inquisitive. They used to pick up the phone when it rang and he used to say 'Come up to me flat and I'll give yer a fiver' and all this. It was obviously in these flats here. Just coming out with filth and abuse. He obviously had a view of the telephone box because if any (kid) was passing the phone started ringing. That was reported time and again . . . dare you let yer children out when it's dark if there's people like that hanging about.'

The control estate

As has been noted, social and economic circumstances of the residents of the Hull control estate somewhat improved over the period relative to the residents of the experimental estate. As with the London control estate, and in many other local authorities over the period, there was some movement towards decentralising housing services but this was neither intensive, estate-based, nor did it conform closely to many of the patterns PEP espoused. The only environmental works on the control estate involved the demolition

61

of some vandalised and unused garages and the enclosure of the entrances to the small blocks of flats. Thus there was little significant change in management, environment or tenant involvement over the study period.

Conclusion

Like other problem estates (cf. Reynolds, 1986) the Hull experimental estate was socially fragmented. The established tenants had managed to insulate themselves, by and large, from the remainder who were generally more vulnerable to adverse economic and personal experiences and misfortunes. Amongst the vulnerable tenants could be found a number of crime-prone groups: networks of adults stealing and receiving stolen goods, and unruly teenage groups who caused trouble far beyond their numbers. Changes in environmental design, tenant consultation and population characteristics —the latter as a result of tenant allocations—occurred during the study period, interacting with each other and with the pre-existing estate culture. The physical changes helped create different levels of vacancies in different parts of the estate and, given the worsening financial circumstances of the newcomers, the populations in the different parts of the estate diverged. Both the design improvements, and the general sense of optimism generated by PEP, gave support to the more stable and established tenants who began to exude a greater confidence about the estate and the possibility of improvement. Yet at the same time, the greater numbers of young poor people and those discharged from institutional care coming onto the estate constituted a destabilising influence, swelling the numbers of vulnerable tenants and encouraging more disorderly activities and lifestyles. Thus both positive and negative developments occurred during the study period. The consequences which the interaction between these tendencies had for criminal activity on the estate is explored in Chapter 8.

7 The London experience: stability

Chapter 3 demonstrated that while residents on the London PEP estate faced serious victimisation risks similar to those on the Hull PEP estate, crime was not seen by residents as a particular problem, largely because the estate was less disorderly than Hull and there was no sizeable, or threatening, youth presence.

Chapter 4 described the mixed but largely disappointing experiences of the tenants on the London experimental estate during the implementation of PEP. On the one hand, improvements were made to the cleaning, caretaking and repairs services, but on the other hand, the difficulties with the housing team leader, the withdrawal of PEP's resources from the estate, and the lack of proper consultation were a disappointment to the tenants. Additionally, a number of those involved in the tenants association who were active before PEP came to the estate became disillusioned, and the local home beat police officer, who was well-liked and supported by residents, was transferred and not effectively replaced. Thus, what might have been promising foundations for informal community control on the estate, were not built upon. Residents' assessments of their estate at the end of the research were mixed, aside from the more positive responses of the relatively small group of Bengali tenants who were helped by the PEP consultant (Chapter 5).

Changes in crime, fear of crime and disorder

Victimisation of the London experimental estate from all types of household offences—as estimated by the household surveys—declined by 26 per cent, burglary fell by 55 per cent, and theft from motor vehicles by 25 per cent. At first glance these results appear promising but as Table A.2 (in Appendix 3) shows, the rate of decline in victimisation was either significantly less—for burglary and total household offences—or the same as that of the *control* estate, which experienced a remarkable decline in crime over the study period. On the control estate, the proportion of households who had been victimised from household offences fell by 50 per cent, victimisation from personal offences fell by 75 per cent and victimisation from burglary by 79 per cent. Since the logic of the research design requires *greater* reductions on the experimental estate relative to the control estate, these findings are enough to negate any *specific* PEP contribution to the reductions in crime on the experimental estate, even though these latter seem substantial.

Additionally, there was no significant difference in rates of change between the estates in residents' feelings of safety whilst walking alone on the estate after dark or of worries about becoming the victim of specific types of crime.

63

There was a significant relative reduction on the experimental estate in residents' perceptions of environmental incivilities—presumably reflecting the success of the caretaking staff in cleaning up the estate and discouraging vandalism—but this was accompanied by a relatively greater increase on the experimental estate in residents' perceptions of person-related disorderliness.

Change on the control estate

So what happened on the control estate? Unfortunately, limited research resources meant that the control estate could not have been the subject of detailed ethnographic research and it is thus difficult to know exactly why such dramatic reductions in crime occurred in the absence of any purposive crime prevention action. Nevertheless, the research team was kept informed officially of developments during the project through its Research Advisory Group—which contained officials from the Tower Hamlets Neighbourhood in which the control estate was located—and the before and after survey data also contain relevant information. From these albeit limited data sources it is possible to hazard three explanations from the reduction in crime: i. improved housing management; ii. increased physical security; and iii. an increase in social control.

i. improved housing management

The study of housing service delivery (Glennerster and Turner) also kept track of developments on the control estate. Table 11 taken from this part of the research, compares the implementation of the various elements of the PEP model between the two estates. It can be seen that, in many respects, much of the recommended PEP model had also been implemented on the control estate. To some extent, the convergence between the two is to be expected—the PEP model was, after all, being commended to local authorities as an exemplary model of an intensive approach to the desirable goal of decentralisation and it is a mark of successful dissemination that it should be adopted in a routine manner in other, 'non-special' estates. In view of the disappointing early performance of the housing team leader on the experimental estate and the consistently good housing management of the control estate, it may not be surprising that many of the ingredients of PEP were actually *better implemented* on the control estate. Additionally, throughout the study period, the tenants were reported to have had good day-to-day relations with the housing management. In part, this was helped by the existence of a relatively effective tenant organisation on the estate, benefitting from the active involvement of some younger tenants who were in professional occupations.

Thus one possible explanation might be that the control estate actually got a *better* version of many of the ingredients of the PEP model—implemented by its local housing management—than did the experimental estate which, although benefitting from the extra presence of a PEP consultant and an estate-based office, suffered in the early part of the implementation from poor quality housing management. Indeed it might be argued that a PEP-type 'package' of measures, however implemented, was responsible for the reductions in crime on both estates.

Table 11
Implementation of the 'PEP model' on the London experimental and control estates (June 1990)

Elements of the model	Experimental estate	Control estate
1. An estate-based office	operational	local but not estate-based
2. Local repairs team	for some repairs	for some repairs
3. Local allocations	local but not estate based	local but not estate based
4. Local control of rent arrears	centralised collection neighbourhood control	as experimental estate
5. Estate based caretakers and cleaners	yes	yes
6. Tenants actively involved	some progress	success in consultation but not in day-to-day management
7. Capital improvements	largely successful	successful, progressing
8. Staffing	up to recommendations	same
9. Team leader	competent*	same
10. Estate budget	begun	begun

*Note: this evaluation was of the second team leader (see Chapter 4).
Source: Glennerster and Turner.

ii. increased physical security

Parts of the control estate also benefitted from substantial capital improvements which might have had a bearing on crime levels, including lobby and access improvements, door systems, lifts and entry phones to a number of the blocks. The underground garage area which had been burned out previously was refurbished and its unallocated spaces leased for use by the employees of a nearby private company and patrolled by security guards. Again, these changes may have increased the security of the estate as a whole.

iii. an increase in social control

Chapter 2 suggested that an increase in residents' informal surveillance of their neighbourhood can be a deterrent to crime. Table 12 shows a significant increase ($p. < .05$) in the ease with which strangers could be identified on the experimental estate, though the other indicators of informal control remain constant. However, there were also significant increases ($p. < .05$) in the proportions of residents on the control estate who had their neighbours watch their property while they were out, who said they felt responsible for the area just outside their homes by keeping it clean and keeping an eye on it (i.e.

'territoriality'), and who found if very or fairly easy to tell a stranger from someone who lived in the area immediately around their home. It is therefore possible that high levels of residential surveillance on the experimental estate and significant *increases* in surveillance and territoriality on the control estate may have been in part also responsible for the reduction in crime.

Table 12
Changes in informal social control behaviour on the London experimental and control estates.
percentages

	Experimental estate		Control estate	
	pre	post	pre	post
Territoriality	78	78	74	83
Ease of identifying strangers	49	61	36	43
Neighbours keep watch over home when out	64	63	55	63
BASE (respondents)	242	268	382	393

Responses weighted by the number of adults per household

The changes in residential surveillance were particularly marked amongst the Asian residents of both estates. Table 13 shows that—with the exception of territorial activity on the experimental estate—Asian residents on both estates showed greater increases in surveillance than did whites and—with the (understandable) exception of being able to identify strangers—by the end of the study period had reached the white residents' level of surveillance. The proportion of Asian residents increased on both estates and it is possible that it was their additional contribution to the surveillance of the estates which was in part responsible for the decline in crime, particularly on the control estate where Asians were in greater numbers. For example, in the first survey, Asians who had their neighbours watch their property amounted to 11 per cent of the population of the control estate; this figure increased to 25 per cent of the estate population by the second survey, with Asians thus making a greater contribution to the overall level of surveillance on their estate.

Table 13
Changes in informal social control behaviour on the London experimental and control estates: 'Asians' compared to 'Whites'—percentages

| | Experimental estate | | | | Control estate | | | |
| | Asians | | Whites | | Asians | | Whites | |
	pre	post	pre	post	pre	post	pre	post
Territoriality	100	83	78	75	64	82	80	85
Ease of identifying strangers	22	47	49	66	17	38	44	48
Neighbours keep watch over home when out	15	63	69	67	36	62	65	65
as % of population	7	17	73	58	30	41	57	44
BASE (respondents)	13	36	194	189	89	122	265	245

Responses weighted by the number of adults per household

In conclusion, while a specific PEP effect on crime cannot be discerned on the London experimental estate, the fact that crime rates reduced substantially on both estates points to crime reduction factors which both estates might have shared. The magnitude of the reductions must rule out any general area effect occurring in Tower Hamlets and points to particular circumstances on the estates. Tentatively, the evidence would seem to suggest that the control estate got *more* of the beneficial improvements that have been associated with PEP—for example, better housing management, building security, and residential surveillance (see Chapter 2)—than did the experimental estate. These came about on the control estate without the specific intervention of PEP and without the problems which attended PEP's involvement on the experimental estate.

Changes over time in crime on the experimental estate

Despite a lack of evidence concerning the overall impact on crime of the PEP-led initiatives, there were suggestions that the actual *presence* of housing officials and home beat police officers on the experimental estate could have helped to control crime and disorder there. Their impact is best illustrated by what happened during periods when they were absent from the estate. Chapter 4 described the circumstances which led to the withdrawal of the PEP consultancy from the estate during the Summer and Autumn of 1988. PEP's withdrawal occurred at a time when the tenants association had become inactive and demoralised (Chapter 5) and when the popular home beat police officer (Chapter 3) had moved on to another post.

Even though the relationship between tenants and the housing staff was often strained, the estate-based presence of local authority staff may have introduced an additional and visible element of control, particularly when combined with good beat policing. The particular police officer in question felt she had some deterrent effect, suggesting that offenders were highly

67

attuned to her presence and that 'things started to happen' when she and her partner had not patrolled the area for a few days. When she moved on, two young officers took over the beat but, due to competing demands on police time in the neighbourhood, and the small degree of 'crime work' (i.e. arrests and calls for service) the estate generated, spent very little time there.

Until the withdrawal of PEP, the collapse of the tenants association, and the curtailment of a regular police presence on the estate, the tenants were confident that some official channels existed for dealing with problems on the estate even if they chose more often to use informal sanctions (i.e. talking to the offenders themselves) or a mixture of formal and informal sanctions (i.e. enlisting the home beat officer's support to have a 'quiet word' with, for example, troublesome young people). However, when these more formal avenues were temporarily removed, their informal sanctions may have carried less weight as they could no longer convincingly deploy threats to report people to the housing office or call the police.

The ethnographic research found at the time of PEP's withdrawal that crime had become a prominent topic of discussion on the estate: 'there's a lot of illegal things going on . . . at the moment' a tenant said then—which included a spate of burglaries committed by someone who lived on the estate. The crime figures support the tenants' perception that burglaries had increased: 11 burglaries on the estate were reported to the police in 1987 and 18 in 1988. The fact that tenants perceived a change in the level of criminal activity, when the overall number of burglaries remained very low, suggests that the tenants had discerned even relatively small changes in the levels of crime on their estate. Chapter 4 also noted that the repeated environmental survey conducted by Glennerster and Turner registered that environmental abuse was 53 per cent higher during the Summer of 1988 than it had been at the start of the year.

However, when PEP resumed work and the estate office began to function effectively, both environmental disorder and burglaries declined. The environmental survey showed that graffiti, for instance, dropped by 25 per cent between October 1988 and January 1989 (when the local office with its new team leader were again fully functioning)—a level which was maintained through to October 1989. Also during 1989 no burglaries were recorded between June and September but in October when the office was closed due to a strike, three burglaries were reported. Levels of graffiti also increased by 15 per cent between July and October 1989, falling by 19 per cent and stabilising at this level until June 1990 at the end of the study period.

The fact that crime and disorder increased when the estate office was closed only to decline again once it re-opened suggests that the physical presence of local authority staff on the estate might in itself act as a deterrent to crime and anti-social behaviour because it may be clear that officials of the council will take immediate action to report offenders to the police or local authority (depending on the offence) if they witness criminal acts. Indeed, on the experimental estate one of the estate officers actually apprehended a burglar trying to break into a flat. These events suggest that burglars may be acutely sensitive to changes in the level of formal social control and that this may be a factor in their choice of targets.

Some of the flats occupied by Bengali households on the estate seemed to experience a high degree of victimisation (both personal and property offences) while others had not been victimised at all. In terms of burglary, this trend might be explained by the fact that certain floors and particular blocks were more vulnerable than others. As many of the Bengalis were allocated flats as a consequence of being on the Council's homeless register they tended to find themselves in properties which had experienced a greater degree of tenant turnover. The location of an individual property in itself might increase the likelihood of victimisation. For example one of the ground floor flats on the estate was allocated to a Bengali woman. She suffered from repeat victimisation in this property, but when she moved to a flat on the second floor of the opposite block she experienced no further problems. Although a number of factors might have contributed to the harassment ceasing (the fact that ground floor flats are most accessible and that she had other Bengali family and friends close by on the second floor) there is some indication that the flats themselves rather than their occupants might be vulnerable. For example, a fireman and his girlfriend, both white, moved into a corner ground floor flat. They were burgled twice in six months, experienced a number of attempted burglaries, the woman experienced threats and intimidation, and their moped was stolen from the doorstep.

It is possible also that certain properties are more vulnerable because some residents may have weak neighbourly support networks (cf. Forrester *et al*, 1990). The Bengalis for example often had limited interaction with their immediate white neighbours and might have been excluded from the 'watching' activities which occurred. Despite the 'empowerment' of Bengalis as a whole on the estate (Chapter 4), analysis of the survey data revealed that Asians in 1990 on the experimental estate were significantly less likely to have contact with their immediate neighbours than were Asians on the control estate (t=−2.303, p<.05). Possibly, in view of the larger Bengali population on the control estate, more of their immediate neighbours would have been Bengali. Bengalis on the experimental estate may have been perceived to be a vulnerable group by offenders, and therefore constituted an easy target.

Sometimes, design and limited natural surveillance increased the likelihood of victimisation too. For example, despite there being a large number of elderly tenants on the ground floor of the main blocks—who were neighbourly and frequently observed people from their flats—it was difficult for them to 'keep an eye' on the properties adjacent to them because doorways were recessed. Furthermore, these same flats were not clearly visible from the opposite side of the estate due to a large grass mound obstructing the view.

69

Conclusion

Crime reduced on both estates. The scale of the reductions especially on the control estate, illustrates the volatility of crime rates in small residential areas. Quite sharp changes in crime and disorder on the experimental estate, occurring at times when the local office was inactive, also illustrate the highly localised nature of crime on the estates. The much greater decline in crime on the control estate than the experimental estate may have been due to a combination of good locally-based housing managers—themselves implementing many of the ingredients of the PEP package—increased physical security, and greater residential surveillance, stemming in part at least from the stabilising influence of a substantial Bengali community on the estate. Yet as Chapter 5 also showed, on the experimental estate too, the doubling of the estate's Bengali population seems to have been accomplished without any hostile reaction from other tenants, thanks to the efforts of PEP to empower them and the protection which this afforded.

The size of the crime reductions on both estates is compelling enough to afford some optimism that intensive, estate-based action might have some impact on crime. Yet, the early experiences of the experimental estate, particularly concerning the first team leader, illustrate how crucial are good quality housing managers to implementing the PEP package of measures. The sense of lost opportunity on the experimental estate is even greater in view of the initial optimism and enthusiasm of many of the tenants at the outset. The collapse of the original tenants association in the wake of PEP's withdrawal from the estate and the (temporary) closure of the local office indicates a dashing of enthusiasm which may not have been fully recovered, despite the subsequent efforts of the housing team and its new leader. Arguably, the gap between the crime rates of the experimental and control estates measures what might have been attained had tenants' early expectations not been so undermined.

Nevertheless, although intra-neighbour tensions remained on the experimental estate—which saw a relatively greater increase in residents' worries about person-related disorder than on the control estate—neither estate had a significant, nor threatening, youth presence and such criminality as there was amongst adults was confined to activities off the estate. As such, the failure to energise all sections of the estate community may not have had particularly harmful consequences. In contrast, as the next chapter shows, despite in many ways an exemplary implementation of the PEP model on the Hull experimental estate (see Chapter 4), the development of a troublesome youth presence can have serious consequences.

8 The Hull experience: conflicting forces[1]

Chapter 6 described the 'social fragmentation' of the Hull experimental estate and how incoming tenants—who were more often young, single and poor—were concentrated in particular parts of the estate, especially in a group of three tower blocks. Substantial improvements in design, housing services and tenant consultation had also taken place and these interacted with the changing estate population. This chapter shows that although the resulting picture was complex it was nevertheless possible to discern both an intensification of control *and* a simultaneous intensification of criminality on the experimental estate.

Between 1987 and 1990, crimes recorded by the police increased on the estate: there were 383 crimes recorded during 1987; rising to 428 in 1988; and 506 in 1989. In the first six months of 1990 (by the time of the second survey) the total of recorded crime had already reached 306. However, the changing pattern of crime during the study period was considerably more complex than this—the increase in crime was by no means uniform, and some tenants and parts of the estate experienced actual reductions in their risk of victimisation which could be attributed to the changes brought about by the PEP intervention.

Changes in recorded crime

Data collected and analysed by Davidson (1991)—and—represented in Table A.4 of Appendix 3—compares percentage changes in recorded crime levels for the houses and flats on the experimental estate with changes in offence levels for the wider police beat area which more or less covers the entire area of public housing of which the experimental estate is a part. Davidson's analysis found that recorded crime rates on the experimental estate between 1987 and 1990 remained below those of the beat area as a whole but increased at a faster rate over the study period. Within the experimental estates, the houses had crime rates about average for the beat area and the flats had much lower rates. Burglary (dwelling) increased less rapidly than other crime on the estate, but this concealed a high increase in the flats and an actual decline in the houses. Reported incidents of criminal damage increased at a higher than average rate, especially for the houses. The rate of increase in autocrime was less than for the wider area as a whole but was especially marked for the flats. This analysis directs attention to understanding the separate experiences of the house—and flat dwellers over the study period.

71

Changes in social control and disorder

Despite the increase in recorded crimes on the experimental estate over a study period, Table A.5 (Appendix 3) shows a highly significant reduction *relative to the control estate,* in both burglary prevalence (i.e. the proportion of residence burgled during the previous year) and incidence (i.e the per capita rate of burglary victimisations). Table A.5 shows that the size of the relative reduction in burglary was primarily due to the size of the increase in the offence on the control estate—survey–recorded burglary levels remained more or less constant on the experimental estate but more than doubled on the control estate. The relative reduction in burglary was accompanied by relative increases in theft from motor vehicles (both incidence and prevalence) and in the mulitiple victimisation of offences against the person—i.e. a relative increase of incidence but not prevalence of personal offences.

Though the survey analysis revealed that tenants did not feel any less fearful of going out on the experimental estate alone at night, there was a significant relative reduction in the extent to which residents of the experimental estate were worried about becoming the victim of specific types of crime ($t=-5.112$, $p. < .01$). In addition, relatively fewer residents perceived as problems 'environmental disorders' such as graffiti, vandalism, litter etc. ($t=-2.227$, $p. < .05$).

These generally positive results were accompanied by others consistent with a growth in social control and lent support to the crime reductive consequences of improved estate management, as fostered by PEP. For example, there was an increase in tenants perceiving that they now had more 'say' in what happened on the estate ($t=+3.330$, $p. < .01$)—undoubtedly a reflection of PEP's efforts at tenant consultation and the success of establishing a directly elected Neighbourhood Management Committee. Despite a higher rate of turnover, there was also a relative increase in the number of other households on the estate where respondents had friends ($t=+2.262$, $p. < 01$)—though, as noted below, this increase in familiarity can have both positive and negative consequences. More directly related to crime and the growth of community control, there was an increase in 'territoriality' i.e. feelings of responsibility for the area outside the home ($t=2.719$, $p. < 01$)—and in the ease with which stangers on the estate could be indentified ($t=+2.312$, $p. < 05$)—both consistent with Newman's (1972) definition of territoriality.

Nevertheless, there were also simultaneous signs of increasing crime and disorderliness. Generally, there was a relative increase in residents' perceptions of 'person-related disorders' as problems, including disturbances from youths, noisy neighbours, people hanging around drinking, and so on ($t=+2.6436$, $p. < 01$). There was also a growth in tolerance of some forms of disorderly behaviour such as holding noisy parties ($t+=2.093$, $p. < 05$),

72

swearing in the streets (t=+2.486, p.<01) and hanging around in groups (t=+2.198, p.<05). Thus, at the level of the overall community, there appears to be a paradox—signs of increasing control but also signs of increasing disorder. However, ethnographic and survey analysis *within* the estate community reveal the pattern of these conflicting cultural tendencies and, especially, how they were shaped by changes in environmental design, tenant mix and management quality.

The intensification of control

i. the improved area of houses (Area A)

Table 14 illustrates how the physical partitioning of the experimental estate interacted with the pattern of tenant turnover to shape changes in the burglary prevalence rate between different parts of the estate. In the improved area of houses (Area A, see also Figure 3, Chapter 6) there were relative net reductions in victimisation both from burglary (t =-4.374, p.<01) and vandalism to household property, including motor vehicles (not shown, t =-2,449, p.<05) which were significantly greater than in other parts of the estate as well as on the control estate. The monthly observational survey of environmental problems carried out by Glennerster and Turner also shows a very clear divergence in scores by small area. The areas in which environmental works had been undertaken by the time the final survey was administered (June 1990) showed a marked decline in environmental nuisance.

Table 14
Changes in burlgary prevalence and tenant turnover on parts of the experimental estate

Area	burglary(%)[1]			new residents(%)[2]		
	before	after	change	before	after	change
A. improved area of houses	26	12	−14	33	13	−20
B. unimproved area of houses	14	13	−1	22	24	+2
C. three tower blocks	4	26	+22	24	44	+20

[1]. Percentage of households burgled one or more times in past year. Adjusted probabilities controlling for number of adults in household and age of respondent 16-30 years. Logit regression: n=2,128, d.f.=15, deviance (−2log(LO/L1)=1,355, p. <01).

[2]. Percentage of respondents living on the experimental estate less than three years. Adjusted probabilities, weighted by number of adults in household, Logit regression: n=2,128, d.f.=11, deviance (−2log(LO/L1)=4,085, p.<01).

Whereas prior to the improvements, burgled houses in this area (Area A) were more likely to be those that were unoccupied for parts of the day (d.f. 97, t = −2.116, p.<.05), occupancy ceased to be associated with the risk of burglary following the design changes, despite a statistically significant relative increase in the proportion of residents leaving their homes unoccupied. Thus, consistent with the idea of a physical environment

73

providing offenders with opportunities for crime (Clarke and Mayhew, 1980), it would seem plausible to assume that the reduction in accessibility to dwellings produced by the design changes may have been sufficient to counter the risk of burglary in leaving homes empty. During an interview, one resident, who admitted to having committed a dozen or more burglaries on the estate, said that houses with front gardens made it less easy to see whether there was anything worth stealing. Previously, offenders could look directly into front windows while to all intents appearing simply to be walking down a common footpath. The creation of fenced front gardens not only created an area of 'private space' for residents which reduced opportunities for burglars but may also have increased their occupants' territorial influence—compared to the control estate and to other parts of the experimental estate, residents in the improved area of houses (Area A) showed increased responsibility for the area just outside the home (t = +2.3912, p.<.05). As one tenant said: 'people have said to me "I feel a lot safer now" whereas before you never knew who was passing your front at all . . . it's so much quieter . . . the fence is like security to them and they know that if anybody does stray that they've no right to be there if they don't know them'.

ii. the unimproved area of houses (Area B)

Notwithstanding a lack of defensible space, there was also a significant relative reduction in burglary (−2.7456, p.<0.1) in the *unimproved* area of houses—Area B—despite an increasingly disadvantaged resident population in this part of the estate. This area also saw a greater relative increase in residents' territorial behaviour (t = +2.6033, p.<.01). This change in residents' defensiveness may be attributed to the community development effects of PEP since it was accompanied by an increase in other indicators of positive community activity—there was a relatively greater increase in this area in the proportion of residents who thought they had a greater say in what happened on their estate (t = +3.4287, p.<.01), along with relatively greater participation by residents in voluntary activities and organisations on and off the estate (t = +3.4976, p.<.01) and in the number of households in which residents had friends living (t = +2.7258, p.<.01)—despite a high proportion (38 per cent) who had been living on the estate for less than three years.

Physical improvements to the estate and the quality of consultation seemed equally important in the intensification of control. Tenants in the improved area of houses (Area A) were most defended—for obvious and tangible reasons—but the greatest increase in tenants' optimism about the future of the estate occurred in the unimproved area of houses (Area B), where nearly twice as many residents (73 per cent) thought the estate would continue to improve over the next two years as in the improved areas (38 per cent).

The intensification of criminality

i. the three tower blocks (Area C)

At the start of the study period, the three tower blocks (Area C) had a low annual rate of burglary (Table 14) and a stable and predominantly elderly population. By the end of the period, getting on for half the population had changed, with a transient, youthful population and a burglary prevalence rate of 26 per cent (Table 14). Although burglary increased in the three tower blocks at no significantly greater rate than on the control estate, the magnitude of the increase in both areas was considerable. Table 15 also shows how burglary victimisation on the estate, uncovered from the surveys, increasingly concentrated during the study period in the three tower blocks—a pattern which Davidson's analysis—quoted above—also found in the pattern of police recorded burglary incidents. Furthermore, the environmental survey also found that average scores for rubbish, graffiti and property damage in an area around one of the three tower blocks doubled—from 7/100 in July 1988 to 14/100 in June 1990—with most of the rise occurring after the summer of 1989 about the time that the young single people were moving in in greater numbers, and becoming more concentrated, in these tower blocks.

Table 15
Change in the share of burglaries between the different areas of the Hull experimental estate
Percentages (number of respondents) estimated by household surveys

Area	Description	percentage share of burglaries		
		before	after	change
A.	improved area of houses	41	16	−25
		(103)	(107)	
B.	unimproved area of houses	41	44	+3
		(193)	(200)	
C.	three tower blocks	9	33	+24
		(158)	(149)	
D.	the single tower block	7	5	−2
		(58)	(54)	
E.	the smaller blocks	1	1	0
		(66)	(65)	
Number of burglaries		70	75	
		100%	100%	
BASE (respondents)		578	575	

Note:
Burglary includes attempted burglaries

As in most local authorities, high-rise flats in Hull were deemed unsuitable for families with children. They tended therefore to be allocated to adult-only households, including single-adults either living separately or sharing accommodation. The tower blocks had for some years been receiving single young people but during the study period their numbers increased as the older residents moved out, some to the smaller blocks on the estate. The result was an increasing *concentration* of the youthful poor in these blocks.

Many of the incoming young people were unemployed, found it difficult to manage on their benefit payments and quickly got into debt. A clash of life-styles was evident with the remaining, predominantly elderly,

75

co-occupants of the flats who complained of noise and nuisance, graffiti-strewn landings, the anti-social hours many of the youngsters kept, and the deviant activities in which some were engaged. Many of these young people had come from unstable backgrounds and the lack of control and support once they were allocated flats gave rise to considerable problems. Some flats were extensively damaged and became a magnet for other disaffected youth. As the older tenants moved out, they were replaced by more young single residents. In addition to the youngsters, older single persons released from institutions with histories of mental illness or alcohol problems were also allocated flats. This group had very little support, were often exploited by other tenants and sometimes themselves became involved in crime.

Although many of the new young poor coming onto the estate had problems adapting to life in a conventional sense, their experience was far from isolating. At the outset of the study, adolescent 'gang' members on the estate tended to be distinct from the adult criminal networks (Chapter 6) but as the young people moved into the tower blocks on the estate, they began to form links between the estate adults and adolescents. Members of the adolescent gang started to use the youths' flats in the tower blocks (Area C) to 'hang out' while the youths began to establish or solidify contacts with older persons involved in offending. The consequence was a widening and deepening of the networks of adolescents, youths and adults engaged in criminal activities on the estate. As the local home beat officer said: 'You've got different groups within groups: we've got (the adolescent group) that are on the estate causing mayhem . . . they're out of control and they've got so many associates of criminals on the estate with them. The drunks are another . . . and we've got a couple of ex-cons . . released from prison recently . . that have teamed up and they're doing other jobs on the estate too'.

Particularly troubling was the impact which this deepening criminal network had upon the adolescent/delinquent group. As the home beat officer said: 'It's such a breeding ground . . . It leads up (these lads have progressed) from riding motorbikes and doing shoplifting. (Now) their whole life is channelled to becoming a good burglar. The more they get involved in crime the more they get their associates, their friends (involved). They just seem to attract each other. The crooks on (the estate) seem to have so many associates . . . that if you're looking at one lad who's done a crime he's maybe got twenty other friends who he could give the gear to or go to for help. . . The path is there for crime. Nothing we're doing is stopping that or it doesn't seem to be'. The result was a highly cohesive criminal network which was certainly strengthened, and partly generated by the changes in tenant allocation. Concentrating a number of vulnerable and sometimes troublesome tenants in an area which already possessed a well established criminal subculture and was under considerable social stress, served to intensify criminal activities on the estate and facilitated the assimilation of incoming groups, many of whom could be readily exploited. An intensification—of disorder and crime resulted, particularly centred on Area C—the group of three tower blocks. Drug use also increased, with the developing youth subculture providing a conduit for drug taking among young people on the estate.

The remainder of the estate

There was little significant change occurring amongst the population of the remaining blocks (Areas D and E), comprising about 21 per cent of households on the estate. At the outset, victimisation rates in these blocks were roughly similar to those in the three tower blocks and were maintained at these low levels throughout the study period. There was no appreciable change in their demographic composition or rate of population turnover suggesting a process of demographic replacement. The movement of some of the elderly from the three tower blocks (Area C) into the other blocks of flats (Areas D and E) helped maintain a stable population there, but further destabilized demographic succession in the tower blocks (Area C).

The concentration of victimisation

Apart from an estate-wide increase in theft from motor vehicles, the simultaneous intensification of control seems to have confined a potential escalation of victimisation to those households who may have been closest or most vulnerable to the evolving criminal network. For instance, the relative increase in the incidence but not the prevalence of offences against persons on the estate (Table A.4, Appendix 3) indicates an increase in the repeated victimisation of those already victimised.

This confinement effect is particularly noticeable for burglary—the offence which seemed most responsive to the intensification of control (see Table A.6, Appendix 3).

In the improved area of houses (Area A), lifestyle factors affecting household occupancy were initially linked to increased risk—i.e. youthfulness of the respondent, leaving the house unoccupied regularly for some time during the week. However, increased territoriality in this area appears to have removed these risk factors and, instead, single parent households seemed at the end of the study period to stand out amongst the reduced number of victims in Area A—presumably because such households were newer (Chapter 6), more isolated, and more vulnerable, either from reduced household occupancy or those associating with them (Maxfield, 1987b).

In the unimproved area of houses (Area B), households with children appeared most vulnerable initially. As a result of the various changes in control and criminality, by the end of the study period, the risk of victimisation in the unimproved area of houses (Area B) shifted to young people and single parent households who were presumably more vulnerable

77

by virtue of their lifestyle activities and associates. An analysis (logistic regression) of the interaction between length of residence and single parent status of households in this area revealed that a single-parent household living in this part of the estate for less than three years was five times more likely to be burgled than other households who had been there longer—including other single parent households (d.f. 194, t = 2.383, p. <.05).

The process of allocating young tenants to the tower blocks (Area C) had begun prior to the first survey and even amongst an elderly population with a low overall burglary rate, these youths' dwellings were at greater risk of burglary (see Table A.6, Appendix 3). Again, by virtue of lifestyle and associates, the risk of burglary to adults under 30 and poorer households (often the same) increased substantially. By the end of the study, the risk of burglary for an adult aged 16–29 years was fourteen times more than that for other tower block residents (d.f. 147, t = 3.457, p. <.01).

The escalation of disorder

The latter part of 1989 saw an escalation of disorder on the estate, particularly focused on the tower blocks (Area C). Throughout the implementation of the environmental improvements, local youths had vandalised and stolen from the building works sites. This activity increased towards the end of 1989 and teenagers began regularly to vandalise and set fire to garages and sheds. Stones were thrown at the fire brigade while they were dealing with incidents and fire officers refused to attend the estate unless accompanied by police, who also had missiles thrown at them—including used syringes. As described in Chapter 6, events culminated with a major incident of arson to a flat in one of the tower blocks.

Policing

For a time during the study period, the police allocated a group of officers, independent of the PEP initiative, to tackle crime on the experimental estate but this seems to have had little effect and to have been abandoned. At the outset, the estate did not have any 'home beat' policing (i.e. officers dedicated to policing only the home beat) however one home beat officer was appointed to work on the estate in 1989. In response to tenant demands he attempted to tackle the motorcycle problem on the estate and met with some success. He also helped establish a Neighbourhood Watch scheme in one part of the unimproved area of houses which had arisen out of the optimism generated by PEP. The officer was raised on the estate himself and therefore identified with the tenants to a greater extent perhaps than many of his colleagues. Yet despite the home-beat officer's energetic and sometimes imaginative ideas to stem the motorcycle problem on the estate, and his development of both formal and informal policing methods, there remained a widespread and general distrust of, and lack of confidence in, the police: 'We've got the local policeman. You don't see him very often, when you call even if he's on duty he might be in a different area, (so) they send somebody else who's from a different area ... they're not really that bothered, they don't seem very interested, you know.' Table 16 shows no change in the proportion of tenants who were dissatisfied with 'what the police were doing on the estate these days', who remained the majority (about 60 per cent). There was a slight increase in those who were 'fairly satisfied'—the decline in satisfaction with the police on the control estate may be related to the increase in burglary there.

Table 16
Residents' satisfaction with 'what the police are doing on the estate these days'—Hull estates
percentages

| | PEP estate | | Control estate | |
	pre	post	pre	post
very satisfied	4	3	8	4
fairly satisfied	19	24	34	28
neither	16	14	19	17
fairly dissatisfied	27	25	20	27
very dissatisfied	34	34	19	24
BASE (respondents)	578	575	480	497

Data weighted by number of persons aged 16 years or over in household.

The following comments were typical of many tenants' feelings about the police: 'the policing I don't think's got any better ... they have started sifting amongst the trouble causers ... but we're still back at square one when you ring at 5 o'clock and they're coming at 8 or 9 o'clock or even the next day ... when we've rung up and they've been vandalising the place, if the police had come within half an hour they would have got the kids who were doing it. It's no good coming the next day'. 'The attitude of the police at the moment ... is that they're fed up of the crime on (the estate and in the area) but, I mean, it's their job to try and sort it out. It's the people (of the area) who are fed up of it.' The survey showed there was no significant change in the numbers of incidents witnessed by residents during the period; tenants frequently witnessed criminal acts (Chapter 3, Table 5) but did not report them. One tenant summed it up: 'What's the point of reporting it to the police, they can't do anything ... I had my own car stolen out of the garage ... the house which overlooks my garage on the end of the block, they had an alsatian dog, ... (the) dog warned them that there was something afoot so they came out to have a look, they saw the people breaking into the garage and all they was concerned about was (that) their (own) car was ok'. The same tenant, who challenged the family about why they didn't report what they had seen replied: 'if we had said anything they would have bricked our windows in'.

It is possible that the increased territoriality found amongst residents of the experimental estate only extended to the immediate vicinity of their own property. For whatever reason, the work of PEP failed to prompt any comparable police initiatives on the estate, which, despite having a high rate of crime problems and an evolving estate infrastructure of a local office and active tenants, continued to be policed to the dissatisfaction of a majority of tenants and without much discernible impact on crime.

Crime displacement

Limited household surveys were also conducted in three residential areas adjacent to the experimental estate (Displacement Areas 1, 2 and 3) to ascertain whether any displacement of crime might have occurred as a consequence of PEP's activities. There was little, in fact, to differentiate Displacement Area 1 from the experimental estate proper because it consisted of houses surrounding the experimental estate's single tower block and, although initially outside the PEP scheme, it became fully incorporated into the management structure of the experimental estate during the course of the project. 'Displacement Area 2' was physically separated from the experimental estate by a drainage canal. 'Displacement Area 3' consisted of an older estate of houses in council tenure on the other side of the shopping precinct (see Chapter 6, Figure 3).

The rate of growth in burglary prevalence rates was less than that on the control estate in Areas A, B and Displacement Area 1. In other areas, the burglary growth rate was the same as the control estate, which would mean that burglary increased in absolute terms though not at a rate greater than on the control estate. As Displacement Area 1 was adjacent to the improved area of houses, and became incorporated into the PEP, it would seem reasonable to infer that it shared in the growth of control which occurred in Area A. Above average increases in theft from motor vehicles reported on the experimental estate, seems to have been confined only to victims living in the areas of houses on the experimental estate. The layout of this area—which separated the houses from roads and car parks—may have limited resident's opportunities to keep an eye on their cars and, paradoxically, the fencing which privatised the space around the dwellings may have limited opportunities to survey vehicles still further.

Change in total household offences in all areas was in line with that on the control estate. However, the rate of change in victimisation from offences against persons was greater for residents in the unimproved area of houses (Area B) and in Displacement Areas 1 and 3 than in the improved area of houses (Area A) or the tower blocks (Area C). To interpret this changing pattern it would be necessary to have information on the circumstances which brought victims into contact with offenders, which is not available.

Whatever the complex pattern of change in crime levels between these areas it is clear that the relative reduction in burglary in Areas A and B of the experimental estate—which appears to have been the major effect of

PEP—did not result in an increase in burglary in other areas. It is, however, possible that there was a shift to thefts from the motor vehicles belonging to residents living in these two areas.

Conclusion

The way that events on the experimental estate unfolded provided an opportunity to examine both the independent and the interactive effects of change in the main elements that have tended to characterise the classic 'problem' estate—environmental design, housing management quality and social mix (Chapter 1). In this particular configuration of events, environmental design modifications and improvements in management quality (including tenant involvement) interacted with changes in tenant turnover and allocation to the estate. Their combined effect was to alter the internal 'culture' of the estate to produce an intensification both of social control and criminality which found expression in differences between parts of the estate and various groups of tenants.. This supports the view that the various causal influences on crime on a 'problem' estate tend to interact with one another. This is likely to occur because their effect is mediated by the internal culture of the estate community.

Consistent with other research, the events on the Hull experimental estate illustrate the crucial importance of population change in affecting the community dynamics of a neighbourhood and hence the crime it experiences. In the pulic housing sector, population change is shaped by the mechanisms which allocate particular kinds of tenant to specific estates (Bottoms and Wiles, 1988). Nothing that had been achieved on the experimental estate by the end of the study period managed to halt the turnover of tenants on the estate as a whole. It was not within the scope of the present study to ascertain why the estate received an increasing number of the young poor and, in particular, whether this trend exemplified a growing residualisation of council tenure or the further social polarisation of this estate within the local housing market. However, it did vividly illustrate the socially harmful effects of concentrating such a large number of vulnerable people together in an already stressed environment.

This example also demonstrates how estate-based initiatives can mediate the impact of this kind of population change. A plausible interpretation of the events on the Hull experimental estate is that the environmental improvements in Area A reduced the number of vacancies there because the new defensible space environment was valued by its residents. Therefore, of the incoming residents—who were relatively poorer and less likely to be in two-parent family units—those with children were allocated to the unimproved area of houses (Area B) and those without were housed in the tower blocks (Area C). Social cohesion and 'empowerment' increased amongst the residents of Area B as a result of PEP's efforts to involve them in the improvement of services and estate management—and in the anticipation of the benefits of defensible space to come—but the newly-arrived single-parent families who were housed there stood out as especially vulnerable to crime. Despite the improvements to the security of the tower blocks, and the better management of the estate as a whole, the newcomers to Area C—that is, the young, predominantly childless poor—replaced many of the previous, elderly residents and attracted crime to themselves, both as perpetrators and victims, concentrating crime in their part of the estate. The policy implications of this example, and of the events on the London estate, are taken up in the next, and final,[1] chapter.

---

[1]. Portions of this chapter also appear in Hope, T. and Foster, J. (1992) 'Conflicting forces: changing the dynamics of crime and community on a 'problem' estate'. British Journal of Criminology, Vol. [32]. October. pp. 488-504.

9 Conclusions

This study has been about social change; specifically, it has tried to describe the changes which occurred in two local authority housing estate communities during a period in which Priority Estates Project workers, in partnership with the local authorities and residents, sought to bring about changes in housing management, the decentralisation of housing services and the involvement of tenants in the running of their estates. The focus of this particular report has been on the impact of these efforts on crime, disorder and the quality of community life.

The 'community' of a public housing estate is a complex and diverse entity and, perhaps not surprisingly, the task of interpreting the various changes on the estates in terms of the many influences and events which occurred there during the period has proved equally complex. Though the complexity of social change may bother those who seek simple solutions to social problems, it is nevertheless likely to be the reality which would-be crime prevention efforts must confront. If nothing else, it is to be hoped that this study has illustrated the scale of the task facing efforts to reduce crime rates in disadvantaged and deteriorating communities (for comparison, see also Sampson, 1991; Forrester et al., 1990; Sampson and Farrell, 1990; and Forrester et al., 1988).

It was suggested in Chapter 2 that implementing the various elements of the PEP model on an estate might help the community to exert 'informal social control' over criminal and disorderly behaviour. Four ways of doing this were identified in the PEP model—first, by creating more defensible space and better dwelling security; second, by tackling disorder to maintain a safe neighbourhood; third, by investing in the physical and human 'capital' of the estate; and fourth, facilitating community members control over activities and decisions which affect their residential environment. A number of examples of these efforts were found to have occurred on the experimental estates—in contrast to their comparable 'control' estates—which both the field research and the analysis of survey data suggest did indeed bring about reductions in crime and disorder. Together, these examples suggest that the PEP model does have a real potential for reducing crime.

However, on the estates studied during this research, all of the successes were only partial—they occurred in either one or the other of the experimental estates, or only for particular areas or groups of residents in each estate. This was partly because some groups were easier to reach than others and that the

83

scope of PEP's impact was constrained by underlying and often severe social and economic conditions particularly on the Hull estate. Within the realms of their remit however there were two obstacles to the wider effectiveness of the PEP model on the estates studied: first, the 'quality' of implementation; and second, the instability of residential communities arising from population turnover, social heterogeneity and the 'subterranean culture' within estate communities. A consideration of these obstacles encountered in this particular study may shed further light on some of the issues involved in reducing crime on 'problem' estates.

The quality of implementation

It is rapidly becoming a truism that successful efforts at crime reduction depend crucially upon the quality of their implementation (Clarke, 1992; Heal and Laycock, 1986; Hope, 1985). The experience of the London estate attests to this: at the outset, the concern and relative stability of the estate community promised a fruitful basis on which to develop the PEP model. Regrettably, the goodwill and capacity of the community to participate in change was lost at the start by the unsympathetic approach of the initial housing team leader. That person's successor—though generally regarded as conscientious and competent—had a difficult fight to make-up the damage done at the start. The seeming demoralisation of the tenants was further compounded by the PEP consultancy's temporary withdrawal from the estate—in part as a response to poor quality local management—and not helped by the replacement of a popular and effective home beat police officer with officers who appeared to give relatively less attention to the estate. Not surprisingly, the members of the original tenants' organisation, who at the start seemed keen and enthusiastic, became disillusioned and withdrew from active involvement. The net effect of these implementation difficulties was that many of the elements of the PEP model were actually *better* implemented on the control estate—which benefitted from good quality housing management throughout—than they were on the experimental estate, despite the attentions of PEP and a greater decentralisation of housing services. Partly as a result (the control estate also had more stability), the control estate fared much better in terms of reduced crime.

The study of the delivery of housing services carried out by Glennerster and Turner as part of the broader Department of the Environment/Home Office research project discusses in much detail the implementation of all the aspects of the PEP model as they occurred on all four estates, and there is little point in rehearsing these details here. However, the London experience does contain an important general lesson about the implementation of multi-agency crime prevention efforts, particularly in high crime communities—that is, the importance of the *quality* of those involved.

It turned out that the mere existence of local management, caretaking and repairs teams was insufficient to energise the majority of tenants on the London experimental estate. What may have been called for was an

84

open-minded and amenable response to the emerging concerns of the tenant organisation; without such a response, the tenant organisation could not carry the rest of the estate community along with them in the direction of tenant 'empowerment'. Moreover, the negative responses of the team leader undermined the credibility of both the tenants' organisation and the PEP consultant. Additionally, weakness of leadership from the local housing office and tenant organisation resulted in an inability to engage the interest of the replacements for the home beat police officer and to encourage—or even demand—good quality community policing. Thus, the successful long term community work achieved by the PEP consultancy was with the incoming Bengali tenants who were better organised themselves and able to articulate their demands. Yet, as Chapter 5 concluded, other sectors of the community were becoming increasingly demoralised and apathetic. The lesson from this small example, then, is that collaboration and community organisation—at least at the very local level—may depend as much if not more upon the quality of those involved than upon the organisation structures which are put in place.

Stable communities

Nevertheless, even a combination of good quality implementation and organisational change may not be sufficient to help communities tackle crime and disorder. By most accounts, the quality of the PEP consultant and local housing staff on the Hull experimental estate was excellent, most of the ingredients of the PEP model were well implemented (see Glennerster and Turner), and not only were many of the tenants keen to become involved in the estate but actually began to attain some degree of empowerment through a resident-elected Neighbourhood Management Committee (NMC). Yet there was a worrying increase in crime and disorder, at least in one part of the estate, which was only just being contained at the close of the research.

As noted in Chapter 2, the kinds of problem estate where the PEP model is applied are likely to have high rates of population turnover and to be socially and culturally heterogeneous. These conditions lead to 'unstable' or 'disorganised' communities where–in a 'neighbourhood of strangers' (Merry, 1981)—criminal and disorderly activity of various kinds can take place relatively free from community sanction, even if large sections of the community might privately disapprove. In such communities with little or no suitable facilities for leisure, young people, in particular, are often unsupervised during their spare time and are thus free if they choose to engage in disorderly and delinquent activity. Additionally, there may be little community protection—in the form of neighbourliness and 'natural surveillance'—afforded to certain socially isolated or vulnerable groups—such as ethnic minorities, newcomers, and the female-heads of young, single-parent families—who may become disproportionately victimised from crime. It follows that the capacity of the PEP model to bring about community organisation and involvement may be affected by the rate of population turnover and degree of heterogeneity.

All the estates in this study to a greater or lesser degree were 'stressed'. They had high rates of tenant turnover, deprivation and were socially heterogeneous. These conditions changed on the different estates over the time period in ways which appear to have affected the PEP model's capacity to reduce crime. Paradoxically, it seems that the London control estate achieved the greatest social stability, mainly because the Bengali community ceased to be a minority group and came to comprise a major presence on the estate (see Chapter 7). Arguably, the increased presence of the more socially cohesive Bengalis may have served to reduce heterogeneity amongst the estate community and to have altered their status from a victimised group to one which was able to develop its own informal social control.

Though the numbers of Bengalis increased on the London experimental estate, they still remained a minority. Here, it seems, PEP was able to empower them as a group so that they were able to achieve a 'presence' on the estate greater than their numbers (Chapter 5). Nevertheless, the rate of turnover remained constant and the community as a whole remained socially heterogeneous; and over the period, the tenants perceived that 'person-related' disorderliness had increased on the estate (Chapter 7). What may have saved the London experimental estate from experiencing a greater rise in crime and disorder was its small number of local youths, so that even if the community was unable to exercise informal control, there were in fact a smaller number of people who were in need of such control. Thus, there were only sporadic outbreaks of trouble on the London experimental estate, involving a few individuals, though it was noticeable that disorder did increase on those occasions when the local office was closed (Chapter 7).

The full effect of population change and heterogeneity, however, was seen on the Hull experimental estate. Over the study period, population turnover increased and the estate received a greater number of young, single, poor tenants. This population change appeared to increase the instability of the estate community. Nevertheless, the environmental design modifications, improvements in the quality of housing management and the involvement of tenants—all attributable to the combined efforts of the housing department and the PEP consultancy—proved to be a countervailing influence. The outcome, though, was to *concentrate* crime in a particular part of the estate and upon the young poor themselves (including female single-parents). The implementation of the PEP model did seem to lead to some degree of social stability—particularly amongst the longer-term residents of the houses which had or were about to receive environmental improvements—but this was not extended to the community as a whole. The experience of implementing the PEP model on the Hull estate thus vividly illustrates the interplay of 'conflicting forces'—those leading towards social stability and informal social control, and those leading towards social disorder and a broadening of a 'subterranean culture' in which crime plays a significant part (Hope and Foster, 1992).

The crime preventive effect of PEP

The question therefore arises as to whether the PEP model can be seen as a crime prevention measure. Had the findings from this study clearly shown either a consistently positive or nil effect on crime—then the answer would have been equally certain. But the results *were* ambiguous and contradictory and so must be the answer to the question. The two issues which these examples of the PEP model did not address were, first, the social instability brought about by the allocation of particular tenants to the estates; and secondly, the broadening of the subterranean culture which these allocations appeared to exacerbate. Is it reasonable to have expected the PEP model—by which is really meant the partnership of housing management and tenants which the PEP consultancy forges—to have countered these tendencies?

In the first place, it should be remembered that the 'PEP model' is simply an outline of structures and principles for action, which then have to be filled-out and adapted in each local situation. Other than the consultancy it does not provide resources and, especially, it does not manage estates or compel people to act in particular ways. As Anne Power said (quoted in Chapter 1 above), PEP acts '. . . as a catalyst for change, as arbiter between tenants and council, between central and local management, between politicans and officers and tenants, between the DoE and local authorities, facilitating an autonomous local management and maintenance structure at estate level'. This study focused on only two examples of the PEP model in action and it is possible that in other circumstances the problems encountered—particularly that of allocating the young poor to the Hull experimental estate—might have been circumvented.

The study of only two new PEP estates must of course limit the extent to which the findings from this research can be generalised to other PEP projects. Nevertheless, this research has generated a depth of information which has been obtained from only a few other studies of estate-based initiatives. Further, its combination of a 'quasi-experimental' research design and detailed qualitative research means that one can be reasonably certain of the reliability of its findings. Fortunately, from the research point of view, enough happened on the estates to at least illustrate some of the issues which estate-based interventions must confront, even if other responses would be forthcoming in other circumstances.

Allocations and the social mix

An important question arising from this research is whether the council housing department responsible for the Hull experimental estate could or

87

should have taken action to forestall the concentration of the young poor, in view of the problems which such a concentration—though not, of course, every individual young poor person—caused for the estate. The most worrying aspect of the experience was how quickly the concentration and escalation of problems occurred. It seems that almost half the population of the three tower blocks changed in the space of just three years (Chapter 6). It may simply be that the key actors on the Hull experimental estate—preoccupied with the major task of implementing the PEP model—simply gave little attention to the build-up of youth-crime problems until a crisis had almost been reached. If such a rapid change and escalation had not been anticipated its sudden arrival may have come as something of a surprise to those involved.

Nevertheless, while it would seem obvious to intervene in the process of allocating prospective tenants to the estate in order to forestall the concentration of social problems, it may not prove easy to do so in practice, in part because local housing officials need to pursue a number of policies simultaneously. For instance, the *PEP Guide to Local Housing Management* (Power, 1987b)—which contained the benchmark description of the PEP model used in this research (see also Glennerster and Turner's report)—states that 'where an estate has been stigmatised over a long period and many vulnerable and dependent households have been concentrated together, it may be necessary to encourage a more varied range of applicants and help widen the offers made to desperate cases for other parts of the housing stock (Power, 1987b, Vol. 1, p. 8)'. This clearly gives encouragement to housing officals to develop special lettings policies which aim to manipulate the social composition of estates. The *Guide* also enjoins housing officials to keep dwellings occupied: 'empty dwellings are one of the major deterrents to new applicants and a cause of demoralisation and fear to existing residents . . . local managers have the *strongest possible incentive* to keep all dwellings occupied . . . a reduction in empty dwellings not only helps the rehoused residents, the level of vandalism and repair, and the cost of the service; it offers a general benefit to the estate environment and the *stability of the community* (DoE, 1987, Vol. 1, p. 8, emphasis added).

Housing officials thus need to maintain a balanced social mix on estates while at the same time keeping all dwellings occupied. Being able to do both however, may depend upon the ability to match the vacancies arising on the estate with the needs of prospective tenants. Not only did the Hull experimental estate experience a higher turnover but by the end of the study period it was receiving a much greater number of those in desperate housing need than the control estate: the second household survey revealed that 28 per cent of residents had been on the Hull experimental estate for less than three years—compared with 16 per cent on the Hull control estate—of whom 21 per cent had been formerly homeless (the comparable figure for the control estate was 16 per cent). Despite the efforts to improve the experimental estate, about the same proportion of residents as at the outset said they would move if they had the chance (51 per cent—compared to 46 per cent on the control estate); a third had actually requested a transfer to another estate (compared with a quarter of residents on the control estate); and the proportion of residents who thought that the Hull experimental estate had a bad reputation among people who live elsewhere in the city had risen to 90 per cent (compared to 76 per cent on the control estate). It would seem that the reputation of the experimental estate had worsened over the period, with the consequence that the estate was receiving poorer newcomers with other personal and social difficulties.

Vacancies were, however, occurring differentially across the Hull experimental estate. First, residents of the houses which had benefitted from new fencing had been encouraged to stay, thus in effect reducing the number of house vacancies on the estate. Secondly, the elderly population were moving at a greater rate out of the tower blocks thus increasing the number of flat vacancies. Generally, research suggests that council sector vacancies are higher in areas—like the Hull experimental estate (see Chapter 3)—that contain a high proportion of elderly households and/or single-person households because each is associated with household dissolution (i.e. death or movement into more suitable accommodation due to old age or marriage) which leads to the creation of a vacancy (Kleinmann, 1990). Housing officials were thus faced with the task of needing to let more flats than houses.

It is now general policy for most local housing authorities not to let flats above the ground floor to families with children, in large part because of research showing the deleterious effect of high-rise dwelling on children, and the damaging impact of children on the communal areas of blocks of high-rise dwellings (Wilson, 1978). As local housing officials had 'the strongest possible incentive' to maintain occupancy on the estate, yet were faced with a low demand from council sector transfers and an excess of housing unsuitable for children, they may in practice have had little choice, if they wished to meet all these criteria, than to let the flats to those from amongst the pool of prospective tenants who were in desperate need, whom the council was legally obliged to house, and who were deemed suitable for the available accommodation. As the research shows, these were often the young and poor and single people coming out of institutions. Accommodating them in the tower blocks only further exacerbated the problem since the lifestyles of some of the newcomers served to hasten the departure of even more of the older tenants. In sum, a spiral of deterioration was set in train by this allocation process which appeared to become self-perpetuating. The tragic irony was that the imperative of filling vacant dwellings to maintain the 'stability of the estate' may, in the way that things worked out, have had the opposite effect.

It is beyond the scope of this study to discover why the pool of prospective council tenants in Hull contained numbers of the young poor, and whether they were being disproportionately housed on the experimental estate. Nor

89

can this research suggest a way in which those who make the allocation decisions could stop such a process happening, while simultaneously fulfilling all the necessary and desired criteria of public housing allocation. It is clearly a complex process which involves the weighing of many, often contradictory, considerations. Yet along with other research, this study does underline the crucial importance of housing markets, and tenant allocations, in shaping the community crime careers of council estates (Bottoms *et al.*, 1992).

Conclusion: addressing the 'subterranean culture'

Even if nothing can be done to alter the social mix of problem estates, is a broadening of crime and disorder an inevitable consequence of particular demographic characteristics? The worrying aspect of increasing the number of young poor on the Hull experimental estate was that it also increased the incidence of both offending *and* victimisation. Chapter 8 clearly shows that the risk of victimisation was far higher for the young poor—especially female single-parents—than it was for other residents. In contrast, the risk of victimisation from household offences significantly declined for those living in the improved area of houses. The Hull experimental estate appears to have 'fragmented' socially, with crime—whether offending or victimisation —concentrating around the young poor. Again, this 'concentration effect' seems to have happened relatively rapidly—at least over a three-year period—in part because some of the young persons allocated to the tower blocks appear to have created a 'demographic/lifestyle' bridge between the local adolescent gangs and the networks of older criminals. In effect, a broader and perhaps more cohesive network of offending seems to have spread across the estate. Again as Bottoms *et al.* have observed (1989), once established, such networks can persist over many years.

At the end of the study period on the Hull experimental estate, the various design, management and community development efforts of the PEP implementation had combined to *contain* this growth of crime in one part of the estate. It was not clear how long such containment might be continued without some further intervention. Though housing reform is the main thrust of the PEP model, it is not outside its scope to encourage the development of care and control for groups of tenants in special need, particularly in liaison with other agencies, including employment services, social services, probation and police. Indeed, the establishment of a local estate office and channels of communication with residents would seem in many ways an ideal infrastructure for the successful development of estate-based multi-agency collaboration for both crime prevention and other 'community-wellness' activities.

While there were some instances of informal agency collaboration on both experimental estates—including the interest of the probation service in the Hull experimental estate—there was little evidence during the study period that these would lead to more organised collaborative working. In view of the infrastructure created by PEP, and the evident needs to be addressed on the estates where the model operates, there would appear to be a strong justification for multi-agency collaboration built around the implementation of the PEP model. Such an effort might be able to address the problems of specific groups within estate communities in a more comprehensive way.

The difficulties which can be posed by the 'social mix' on estates are usually well-known to local residents, whose understandable reaction is often to call for the eviction of the 'troublemakers'. As one tenant said: 'there's a lot of decent people living here now. I would think twenty per cent are absolute rubbish. They (the council) have these daft ideas that if they put the bad tenants among the good'uns then the good'uns will drag the bad'uns up to their level. Of course anybody who lives here knows that it goes the other way eventually, the good'uns say (no more) because they're fed up.' It would have been unrealistic to suggest that housing on the Hull experimental estate should no longer have been allocated to the homeless, young single people, or other 'problem' families (much though other tenants might want this), because they need housing and the estate had empty properties available. However, it might have been possible for the local authority to provide a more structured and supportive environment for young people who were already there and those who had yet to move in. Some kind of sheltered scheme for the young, for example, similar to warden-controlled blocks of flats for the elderly or student halls of residence might have worked. The presence of an adult figure, and rules establishing good behaviour, may have helped to contain problems and prevent other youngsters who did not live in the scheme from taking advantage of the residents. Of course, suggestions such as these always need to take their turn with many other pressing demands on limited local authority budgets and often tend to fall by the wayside. Ironically, though, a scheme of this kind had already been tried on two other housing estates in Hull with considerable success.

A proper consideration of how to cope with the needs of, and problems presented, by the young poor on problems presented, by the young poor on problem estates again goes beyond the scope of this report. It is fair to conclude, however, that these needs and problems were not addressed in the cases examined here.

The analyses presented have identified two contrasting or conflicting sets of social processes—those which foster the growth of social control, and those which encourage the growth of criminality. Much crime prevention effort in recent years on problem estates has, in one way or another, concentrated on developing social control, whether through community development efforts or by creating opportunities whereby community members or others (including the police) can exert social control, particularly through the surveillance of the immediate, residential environment. As noted in Chapter

91

2, a principal reason for evaluating PEP from the perspective of crime prevention was that it embodied many of the elements which past experience had suggested would encourage social control; and many aspects of the present research vindicate this assumption.

However, there is much less of a corpus of knowledge and practice which would help in dealing with those factors which encourage the growth of criminality on estates. Indeed, it has often been assumed tacitly that efforts to promote control will, of themselves, also reduce criminality. The experience of the Hull experimental estate, at least, suggests that the processes which helped to widen and deepen the 'subterranean subculture' of crime on the estate occurred more or less independently of those acting to promote social control. Put another way, the greater control which the more established tenants were able to exert extended only to their own immediate residential environment and was essentially 'defensive', that is, working mainly to keep intruders or predators away. There was little sense that the PEP model had helped support the development of social norms against offending (Chapter 2).

If anything, the considerable achievements of the housing department and PEP in implementing major changes on the Hull experimental estate in such a short time may have diverted attention away from the growing problem of youth crime on the estate which the increasing arrival of the young poor intensified. The quotations from tenants on the estate highlight the difficulties residents faced in dealing with troublesome residents, particularly troublesome adolescents. While the research reported here vividly illustrates the problems of escalating youth crime, and the widening subterranean culture which nourished it, it has little to say about how these problems could have been prevented. Answers to these thorny issues require much more creative thought and action. Nevertheless, the research does illustrate both the strengths and the limitations of crime reduction through the promotion of informal social control.

The reality of life on high crime estates is that the 'community' is socially fragmented. As the ethnographic research reported here found, the more established and stable families, from which PEP drew its core of activists, tended to keep themselves apart from the other, more vulnerable residents, especially the troubled and troublesome minorities. Indeed, their concern was to have these groups removed from their estate. In the light of this study, it would seem unrealistic to expect many residents to be able or willing to exert much direct influence over the behaviour of those involved in crime and disorder on the estate. Thus the means to tackle the causes of that criminality which is directed by some residents against others may need to be sought elsewhere.

Conclusion

This study was oriented chiefly towards examining the mechanisms of social control embodied in the PEP model, and it did amass a considerable amount of evidence supporting the tentative model for PEP's effect on crime which was advanced in Chapter 2 (Figure 1). Nevertheless, in the course of the research it became clear that there existed another set of social processes which fostered the growth of criminality on estates. This present study was not designed to explore these processes—though some light was shed on them—nor was it able to investigate the efficacy of any particular means of tackling such estate-based criminality. It nevertheless demonstrates the scope and limitations of informal social control and the need to complement this with a concerted effort to tackle the underlying factors which led to the development of criminal activity.

Appendix 1: Estimating the effect of PEP: the survey analysis

This appendix describes the methodology employed to estimate the effect of PEP on each of the experimental estates.

Survey data

The 'pre' or first survey was carried out in the summer of 1987 prior to the establishment of PEP. The 'post' or second survey was carried out over the same period in 1990. The pre-survey used a two-stage sample design whereby households were selected at the first stage and individuals were selected at random from those households at the second stage. For the post-survey, it was decided that, where possible, the pre-survey respondents should be re-interviewed, thus providing a panel of respondents who had been present on the estate for the full three year period. In addition, it was also necessary to interview a new representative cross-section of the current estate population to enable changes to be measured between the populations of the estates in 1987 and 1990. The sample was therefore selected to be both representative of the current estate population and to incorporate a panel of 1987 respondents.

Individuals were required to give information not only about themselves but also about their household in the interview. All the addresses that were issued—from lists of dwellings supplied by the respective housing departments—for the pre-survey were re-issued for the post-survey. A breakdown of responses by estate is given in Tables 17 and 18. In both surveys, interviews conducted with ethnic minority group members were carried out by an interviewer with the same ethnic background. In the post survey this was considered necessary only for the Asian and Vietnamese residents of the London estates. In addition, for these groups, interviewers were also matched to the gender of the respondent.

Table 17
Survey Responses—Hull Estates

	Experimental Estate		Control Estate		Displacement Areas	
	pre	post	pre	post	pre	post
Set sample	841	841	754	754	767	767
Ineligible addresses (Voids)	55	64	48	41	108	52
Total possible	786	777	706	713	659	715
Final sample	578	575	480	499	427	530
Response rate (as % of total possible)	74%	74%	68%	70%	65%	74%

94

Table 18
Survey Reponses—London Estates

| | Experimental Estate | | Control Estate | |
	pre	post	pre	post
Set sample	439	439	641	641
Ineligible addresses (Voids)	60	19	51	20
Total possible	379	420	590	621
Final sample	242	268	382	393
Response rate (as % of total possible)	64%	64%	65%	63%

Questionnaire

The same questionnaire—with the addition or deletion of a few items—was used in both surveys. The questionnaire was modelled on that used in the British Crime Survey and contained 'screener' questions probing for victimisation experiences and separate 'victim forms' (up to a maximum of six forms per victim). The questionnaire covered respondents demographic characteristics, problems with their dwelling and estate, information on repairs and perception of estate services, witnessing and intervention in crime, experience of victimisation and perceptions and worries about crime, and intentions to move.

Measurement scales

In a number of instances, survey responses were combined into simple additive scales though in some cases the decision to combine individual survey items was taken on the basis of a Principal Components Analysis (PCA). The main scales were:

i. physical (environmental) disorder

Each of the following list of items was coded: big problem = 3; something of a problem = 2; not a problem = 1. Scale items were selected by PCA and included: lack of safe play areas for children; rubbish and litter lying around; dog mess; unattended dogs; graffiti; broken street lighting; empty houses/flats; secure car-parking; and broken down and abandoned cars. Individual scores on each of these items were added together.

ii. social (person-related) disorder

The scale was constructed as above. Items included were: disturbances from teenagers and youths; noisy parties; noisy neighbours apart from noisy parties; noisy people outside your home; people mending cars and bikes outside your home; people who say insulting things or bother people as they walk down the streets; people using illegal drugs; speeding traffic; people hanging around drinking.

95

iii. worry about crime

Respondents were asked how worried they were about being the victim of the following different types of crime on the estate: having your home broken into and something stolen; having your home or property damaged by vandals; being attacked or robbed while on the estate; being racially harassed or abused while on the estate; being insulted or bothered by people on the estate; and (for women only) being raped or sexually assaulted while on the estate; and being sexually pestered while on the estate. Items were coded: very worried = 4; fairly worried = 3; not very worried = 2; not at all worried = 1. Respondents scores were added and divided by 5 (for males) and 7 (for females) to give an average worry score.

Estimation of the PEP effect

Each pair of experimental and control estates—in London and Hull respectively—were analysed separately. The cross-sectional survey data from both waves for both estates were pooled and then analysed using multivariate maximum likelihood methods derived from the generalised linear model, as implemented on the GLIM system. The objective for each indicator of effect (or dependant variable) was to construct a statistical model which:

   i. isolated absolute change (i.e. that component of change which each estate shared in common) from relative change (i.e. that additional change which was unique to the experimental estate)

   ii. corrected for possible bias due to inexact matching of experimental and control estates.

Statistical models took the general form:

$$Y_{i..k} = wave + treat + wave.treat + x_{i..k}$$

where:

$Y_{i..k}$ = each individual indicator of effect
wave, 0 = pre-test survey respondent and 1 = post-test survey respondent

treat, 0 = control estate and 1 = the experimental estate.

$X_{i..k}$ = relevant covariates used to match pre and post and experimental and control samples.

wave.treat = the interaction term *wave(1) x treat(1)* denoting a respondent living in the experimental estate interviewed in the post survey.

In the above model, the parameter *wave.treat* indexes those respondents who were present in the experimental sample at the second survey. When the parameters *wave* and *treat* are also included, it can be considered to measure the effect of the PEP intervention, or 'treatment' effect, by comparing the condition of the group indexed by the parameter wave(1).treat(1), from

APPENDIX 1: ESTIMATING THE EFFECT OF PEP: THE SURVEY ANALYSIS

the other four conditions—i.e. wave(1).treat(0), wave(0).treat(1) and wave(0).treat(0). Covariates ($x_{i \ldots k}$), which were demographic characteristics of individuals and their households, were selected by a backward-elmination procedure and added to the models. For a justification of this general method see Judd and Kenny (1981).

The statistical significance of the treatment effect parameter —*wave.treat*—was assessed by $p. = t = c/s.e.$, where t = the t-statistic, c = the estimate of the parameter wave.treat and *s.e.* = the standard error of the estimate. This assesses the extent to which the treatment group— wave(1).treat(1)—differs from the other groups. The same general model was used throughout. Depending on the level of measurement of the dependent variable, different error functions for the generalised linear models (GLMs) were constructed as follows:

binary coded variables (including victimisation prevalence rates)—LOGIT.

interval level variables (ordinary least squares regression)—IDENTITY.

victimisation counts (incidence rates)—LOGARITHM

Estimates (accompanied by their standard errors and/or t-values) are reported either as:

    i. actual parameter values—b.wave(1).treat(1).

and for logit models only:

    ii. adjusted probabilities (rates)—Prob(x)—where

        prob(wave(0).treat(0)) = l(a)
        Prob(wave(1).treat(0)) = L(a + $b$wave)
        Prob(wave(0).treat(1)) = L(a + $b$treat)
        Prob(wave(1).treat(1)) = L(a + $b$wave + $b$treat + $b$wave.treat)

and L(.) = exp(.)/(1 + exp(.)).

    iii. relative odds (RO) where

        RO = exp($b$wave.treat).

Appendix 2: Estimating the effect of PEP: the detailed ethnographic observation

In order to evaluate the impact of the Priority Estates Project the *process* of change on the estates was as important as the absolute changes measured by the 'before' and 'after' surveys at two fixed points in time. This required in-depth and detailed observations on the estates to establish:

i. whether PEP had an impact upon crime and community, and, if so, what kind of impact?

ii. whether PEP's work changed the way in which tenants perceived their estate, and whether this resulted in increased informal social control and reduced levels of crime?

iii. what changes, if any, did occur and what was PEP's role in these?

This ethnographic work, described below by the researcher, Janet Foster, was used not only to explain the statistical findings but also to determine particular questions the analysis should address.

The London experimental estate

I spent eighteen months on the London experimental estate between April 1987 and June 1990. Contact was made initially with the housing department and with tenants through the recently established tenants association. As the researcher, I was unable to get accommodation on the estate so I adopted an overt role and told tenants that I would be spending some time on the estate looking at the housing experiment that was being implemented there. I did not mention my interest in crime.

Tenants were very welcoming. They were often surprised that I should be interested in their experience of living on the estate but were always willing to talk and spent many hours over cups of tea and meals chatting about their lives and the changes taking place on the estate.

I regularly observed a variety of different meetings during the course of the research including those of the tenants association, PEP, council, and public meetings where issues concerning the estates were raised. I also attended social events, including the mother and toddlers group, barbecues, and practice sessions for the kids' football team.

As the tenants became accustomed to my presence they found their own ways of explaining it. At a charity darts match between estate residents and the local police I was introduced as 'this is Janet and she's our community lady.'

After several months of observations I conducted interviews, frequently with a tape recorder, with the key members of the tenant group in their homes. I asked them about their experiences of living on the estate, how they had come to be housed there, in what ways it had/had not changed during the time they had lived there and what role they felt the tenants association was playing on the estate. I adopted an unstructured approach leaving tenants to talk about their experiences with as little prompting as possible. They often talked about crime and their experiences as victims without me raising the issue directly.

Once I had interviewed tenants who were actively involved on the estate, I asked them, and all those I interviewed subsequently, to introduce me to someone else they knew on the estate so that I could extend my focus away from those most closely involved with the changes taking place on the estate. This technique is known as 'snowballing'. This revealed what tenants who were not involved, and were often not aware of PEP's presence, felt about the estate and enabled me to establish if any changes were discernible to them.

Over the three year research period I interviewed 45 residents on the London estates, and twenty-five PEP personnel, police officers, councillors and housing staff connected with the estate. Some residents and workers were interviewed twice and occasionally three times during the life of the project.

The Bengali households were interviewed with the help of an interpreter, who was a tenant on the estate. I also tried to make contact with the small Chinese/Vietnamese community but without success.

The Hull experimental estate

I had initially thought that my southern accent would be a considerable disadvantage on the Hull estate. In fact, it was not a problem although people did ask from time to time if I had had elocution lessons. Tenants were amazed that a researcher had come all the way from London to find out about their experiences of living on the estate and as a result were very willing to help with the research.

I approached the tenant group on the estate as I had done in London and began to attend their monthly meetings. I adopted similar snowball techniques and this was effective for the 'established' tenants but, since networks on the estate were more contained, it did not open up access to the more vulnerable and needy groups on the estate. As a result it took six months before I became aware of the hidden economy activities and was exposed to the subterranean culture described in this report. Perhaps due to the distances from home and the particular nature of the estate itself I was far more reliant on official agencies (Probation, Single Persons Support, and Housing) for introductions to the vulnerable and crime-prone groups than I was on the London estate. I also gained access through the local Outreach centre and the youth club.

I spent a year on the Hull estate between October 1988 and June 1990. In addition to my observations I interviewed 43 residents on the estate and twenty-one people connected with it through PEP, the local police, councillors, Probation and Single Persons Support. As in London, many of these were interviewed twice and sometimes three times during the course of the research.

I also conducted group discussions with students in the local secondary school and administered questionnaires similar to the Home Office survey questionnaire to 131 students between the ages of 11 and 15 who lived on the estate (although only half the sample lived on the part of the estate that was being evaluated).

As it was not always possible for me to be in Hull I asked selected tenants on different parts of the estate to keep diaries for me about things that happened on the estate. These often included personal reflections about events which had taken place.

At the time of the first survey I was already involved in observations on the London experimental estate. During the second survey I observed the survey researchers conducting interviews on both the London and Hull estates. This was a revealing exercise. I was able to observe how the survey was received by residents on both estates and for the second survey I noted down all the qualifying remarks tenants made to questions they were asked, the different ways they were interpreted and the additional, and sometimes important remarks they made in relation to some of the areas discussed by the survey.

There is little doubt that the use of mixed methods in this evaluation was very important. Percentages are frequently given more credence than in-depth observations, but without the contextual information, survey data can be open to distortion and misinterpretation. Similarly ethnographic work will always be open to criticisms if observations cannot be supported by numerical and more generalisable data. In this research both were used.

Appendix 3

ADDITIONAL TABLES
Table A.1
Racially-motivated victimisation in the London estates
Pre- (1987) and Post- PEP (1990)
Maximum likelihood estimates

Dependent variable: number of victimisations no estate which victim said were racially motivated—GLM poisson errors

	Estimate	*s.e.*	*t-ratio*	*sig*
constant	−6.375	0.700	−9.107	●
Asian	4.738	1.053	4.500	●
Vietnamese	0.472	1.035	0.456	—
Experimental estate	0.940	1.228	0.765	—
1990 vs. 1987	−0.165	1.416	−0.117	—
Experimental estate in 1990	2.154	1.600	1.346	—

Compared with Asians on control estate in 1987 (reference category):

Asians on control estate in 1990	−9.148	10.690	−0.856	—
Asians on experimental estate in 1987	−0.239	1.362	−0.175	—
Asians on experimental estate in 1990	−4.105	1.186	−3.461	●

	D.F.	*Deviance*		
Residual	1,268	281.9		

[1]Bulleted t ratios significant at 5 per cent probability level. N= 1,282.

[2]The model also controls for (not shown): whether married/cohabiting; whether in full-time employment; single-parent household; elderly household; and length of residence.

Table A.2
Changes in victimisation on the London estates
prevalence (per cent residents)
incidence (per 100 residents) (bold type)

	victimisation rates				relative change[1]		
	Experimental		Control		estimate	s.e.	sig.
	pre	post	pre	post			
vandalism	11.7	9.7	11.2	8.1	+0.344	0.422	—
	19.4	**15.8**	**18.2**	**16.6**	**+0.0412**	**0.289**	—
burglary	7.6	2.1	8.3	2.7	−0.035	0.570	—
	11.0	**5.0**	**14.0**	**3.0**	**+0.912**	**0.448**	*
theft from motor	22.8	19.0	16.2	9.1	+0.740	0.514	—
vehicles	**30.6**	**23.0**	**21.9**	**14.9**	**+0.255**	**0.369**	—
total household	31.5	25.0	28.4	15.9	+0.709	2.345	*
offences	**61.1**	**44.7**	**64.0**	**31.9**	**+0.531**	**0.162**	**
total personal	**7.8**	**5.5**	**7.7**	**3.0**	**+0.691**	**0.485**	—
offences	11.2	12.6	16.0	4.0	**+1.765**	**0.351**	**

* = p.<.05 ** = p.<.01. N = 1,282.

[1]For definition of the estimate of relative change see Appendix 1. A positive (negative) sign indicates that the rate of change was greater (less) than that of the control estate. The significance test (t-test) indicates that the difference in the rate of change was greater (less) than zero. Each estimate takes into account relevant demographic covariates.

Table A.3
Recorded crime on the Hull Experimental Estate in 1987 compared to the wider area—crimes per 1000 dwellings.
(in parentheses: percentage changes in rates between 1987/89)

	PEP estate		Police beat area	
	flats	houses	total	total
burglary dwelling	44	93	67	83
	(+76%)	(−8%)	(+21%)	(+11%)
criminal damage	30	74	51	63
	(+59%)	(+92%)	(+80%)	(+35%)
autocrime	18	121	66	86
	(+110%)	(+44%)	(+53%)	(+64%)
all reported offences	165	562	354	508
	(+64%)	(+22%)	(+32%)	(+23%)
number of dwellings	569	514	1,083	2,440

Source: Humberside Police and Norman Davidson (1991, Personal Communication).

Table A.4
Changes in victimisation on the Hull estates
prevalence (% residents)
incidence (per 100 residents) (bold type)

| | victimisation rates | | | | relative change[1] | | |
| | Experimental | | Control | | | | |
	pre	post	pre	post	estimate	s.e.	sig.
vandalism	19.4	22.8	12.3	21.2	−0.394	0.243	—
	41.0	**54.8**	**25.9**	**48.1**	**−0.258**	**0.144**	—
burglary	10.3	9.6	6.1	15.4	−1.074	0.298	**
	13.5	**12.7**	**8.8**	**18.1**	**−0.759**	**0.242**	**
theft from motor	20.8	29.4	26.2	22.4	+0.712	0.345	*
vehicles (vehicle	**33.8**	**65.1**	**44.7**	**38.3**	**+0.909**	**0.231**	**
owning hhs.)							
total household	47.4	48.7	43.6	48.0	−0.177	0.189	—
offences	**113.3**	**148.5**	**99.1**	**118.3**	**+0.072**	**0.084**	—
total personal	11.7	11.5	11.3	5.5	+0.334	0.334	—
offences	**22.9**	**35.0**	**23.6**	**12.1**	**+0.643**	**0.183**	**

* = p.<.05 ** = p.<.01. N = 2,128.
[1]For definition of the estimate of relative change see Appendix. A positive (negative) sign indicates that the rate of change was greater (less) than that of the control estate. The significance test (t–test) indicates that the difference in the rate of change was greater (less) than zero. Each estimate takes into account relevant demographic covariates. See Appendix.

Table A.5
Crime movement in and around the Hull experimental estate
—change odds relative to the control estate (control estate = 1.00)

	burglary	theft from motor vehicles	total household crime	total personal crime
			experimental Estate	
improved area of houses (Area A)	0.133	2.395	—	—
unimproved area of houses (Area B)	0.353	2.184	—	2.171
three tower blocks (Area C)	—	—	—	—
			the displacement areas	
displacement area 1	0.286	—	—	10.309
displacement area 2	—	—	—	—
displacement area 3	—	—	—	2.332

N = 3,089. Data weighted by number of persons aged 16 years or over in household. Models also include (not shown) Areas D and E of the experimental estate. Only estimates significantly different from the control estate at the five per cent level are shown.

Note
Table A.5 compares simultaneous changes in crime prevalence levels between the three key areas of the experimental estate (Areas A, B and C) and the three displacement areas (1, 2 and 3). The table is derived from multivariate (logit) statistical models of the pooled data set (i.e. all areas, both surveys) change for each of the offence prevalence rates of a form as described in the Appendix 1. The table presents estimates of relative change—Area (n) + Wave (1)—having controlled for prior differences between the various areas and general change which they all share. However, instead of of presenting the actual estimates of relative change, these are expressed as their exponents which can be interpreted as the 'odds' of change relative to the change which occurred on the control estate. Thus, in Table A.5 a value of 1.00 represents the rate of change in the offence rate which occurred on the control estate. The rate of change in the improved area of houses (Area A) can therefore be interpreted as 86.7 per cent less than on the control estate (i.e. 1.00 – 0.867). Calculation of such odds allows comparison between areas, each standardised by its relationship to the control estate (i.e. the 'reference' category). Only those relative odds are shown which differ significantly (p. <.05) from the control estate.

Table A.6
Changes in the characteristics of burglary victims in different parts of the Hull estate over time (chi-squared values)

| | Parts of the estate | | | | | |
| | improved area | | unimproved area | | tower blocks | |
	wave 1	wave 2	wave 1	wave 2	wave 1	wave 2
New residents	1.008	1.542	0.128	1.717	0.252	2.264
Under 30 years	3.987*	0.364	0.298	6.331*	6.901**	18.223***
Children in household	0.250	0.122	4.041*	2.254	—	—
House sometimes empty	4.444*	0.017	2.817	0.211	0.642	0.635
Lone-parent household	0.611	3.341*	2.622	5.935*	—	—
Household receiving housing benefit	0.116	2.805	0.085	0.469	0.052	4.153*
BASE	103	107	193	200	158	149

Note: Chi-squared values calculated from 2 × 2 frequency tables comparing burglary victims (once or more times in past year) with non-victims. P. <.05 = *; p. <.01 = **; p. <.001 = ***. Children were not accommodated in the tower blocks.

References

Abrams, P. (1986). In Bulmer, M. Neighbours: the work of Phillip Abrams. Cambridge: Cambridge University Press.

Allatt, P. (1984a). 'Residential security: containment and displacement of burglary'. *Howard Journal*, 23, 99-116.

Allatt, P. (1984b). 'Fear of crime: the effect of improved residential security on a difficult to let estate'. *Howard Journal*, 24, 170-182.

Armstrong, G., and Wilson, M. (1973). 'City politics and deviancy amplification'. In Taylor, I. and Taylor, L. *Politics and Deviance*. Harmondsworth: Penguin Books.

Barr, R. and Pease, K. (1990). 'Crime Displacement'. In Tonry, M. and Morris, N. (Eds.). *Crime and Justice: a review of research*. Chicago: University of Chicago Press.

Bottoms, A. E. and Wiles, P. (1988). 'Crime and housing policy: a framework for crime prevention analysis'. In Hope, T. and Shaw, M. (Eds.). *Communities and Crime Reduction*. London: HMSO.

Bottoms, A. E. and Wiles, P. (1986). 'Housing tenure and residential crime careers in Britain'. In Reiss, A. J. and Tonry, M. (Eds.). *Communities and Crime. Crime and Justice: a review of research*, Vol. 8, Chicago: University of Chicago Press.

Bottoms, A. E., Claytor, A. and Wiles, P. (1992). 'Housing markets and residential community crime careers'. In Evans, D. J., Fyfe, N. R. and Herbert, D. T. (Eds.) *Crime, Policing and Place*. London: Routledge.

Bottoms, A. E., Mawby, R. I. and Xanthos, P. (1989). 'A tale of two estates'. in Downes, D. *Crime and the City: essays in memory of John Barron Mays*. Basingstoke: Macmillan.

Bright, J. and Petterson, G. (1984). *The Safe Neighbourhoods Unit Report*. London: NACRO.

Burbridge, M. (1984). 'British public housing and crime—a review'. In Clarke, R. and Hope, T. (Eds.) *Coping with Burglary*. Boston, MA.: Kluwer-Nijhoff.

Centre for Environmental Studies (1984). *Outer Estates in Britain*. London: Centre for Environmental Studies.

Clarke, R. V. (1992). *Situational Crime Prevention: successful case studies*. New York: Harrow and Heston.

Coleman, A. (1985). *Utopia on Trial*. London: Hilary Shipman.

Currie, E. (1988). 'Two visions of community crime prevention.'. In Hope, T. and Shaw, M. (Eds.). *Communities and Crime Reduction*. London: HMSO.

Damer, S. 'Wine alley: the sociology of a dreadful enclosure'. *Sociological Review*, 22, 221-248.

Davidson, N. (1984). Burglary in the community: patterns of localisation in offender-victim relations. In Clarke, R. and Hope, T. (Eds.) *Coping with Burglary*. Boston, MA.: Kluwer-Nijhof.

Davidson, N. (1991). Personal communication to Home Office.

105

Department of the Environment (1981). *An Investigation of Difficult to Let Housing.* HDD Occasional Papers: 3/80 (Volume 1—General Findings), 4/80 (Volume 2—Case Studies of Post War Estates), 5/80 (Volume 3—Case Studies of Pre War Estates). London: HMSO.

Eisenham, P. (1972). In *Architectural Design.* September.

Forrest, R. and Murie, A. (1990). *Residualisation and council housing: a statistical update.* Working Paper 91. Bristol: School for Advanced Urban Studies (University of Bristol).

Forrester, D., Chatterton, M. and Pease, K. (1988). *The Kirkholt Burglary Prevention Project, Rochdale.* Crime Prevention Unit Paper 13. Crime Prevention Unit Paper 13. London: Home Office.

Forrester, D., Frenz, S., O'Connell, M., and Pease, K. (1990). '*The Kirkholt Burglary Prevention Project: Phase II'.* Crime Prevention Unit Paper 23. London: Home Office.

Foster, J. (1990). *Villains.* London: Routledge.

Gill, O. (1977). *Luke Street: housing policy, conflict and the creation of a delinquent area.* London: McMillan.

Gladstone, F. J. (1978). *Vandalism among adolescent schoolboys.* In Clarke, R. V. G. (Ed.) Tackling Vandalism. Home Office Research Study No. 47. London: HMSO.

Greenberg, S. W., Rohe, W. M. and Williams, J. R. (1985). *Informal Citizen Action and Crime Prevention at the Neighbourhood Level.* Washington, D.C.: U.S. Department of Justice.

Heal, K. and Laycock, G. (1986). *Situational Crime Prevention: from theory into practice.* London: HMSO.

Hedges, A., Blaber, A. and Mostyn, B. (1980). *Community Planning Project: Cunningham Road Improvement Scheme.* London: Social and Community Planning Research.

Hope, T. (1986a). 'Council tenants and crime'. *Research Bulletin* 21. London: Home Office Research and Planning Unit.

Hope, T. (1986b). 'Crime, community and environment'. *Journal of Environmental Psychology,* 6, 65-78.

Hope, T. (1985). *Implementing Crime Prevention Measures.* Home Office Research Study No. 86. London: HMSO.

Hope, T. and Roster, J. (1992). 'Conflicting forces: changing the dynamics of crime and community on a 'problem' estate. *British Journal of Criminology,* Vol. 32, No. 4.

Hope, T. and Hough, M. (1988). 'Area, crime and incivilities: a profile from the British Crime Survey.' In Hope, T. and Shaw, M. (Eds.). *Communities and Crime Reduction.* London: HMSO.

Hope, T. and Shaw, M. (1988). 'Community approaches to reducing crime'. In Hope, T. and Shaw, M. (Eds.). *Communities and Crime Reduction.* London: HMSO.

Hough, M. and Mayhew, P. (1985). *Taking Account of Crime: key findings from the 1984 British Crime Survey.* Home Office Research Study No. 85. London: HMSO.

Judd, C. M. and Kenny, D. A. (1981). *Estimating the Effect of Social Interventions.* New York: Cambridge University Press.

Kleinman, M. (1990). The future provision of social housing in Britain. In van Vliet, W. and van Weesep, J. (Eds.) *Government and Housing: developments in seven countries.* Newbury Park, CA.: Sage Publications.

Kornhauser, R. R. (1978) *Social Sources of Delinquency.* Chicago: University of Chicago Press.

Maxfield, M. (1987a). *Explaining Fear of Crime: evidence from the 1984 British Crime Survey.* Research and Planning Unit Paper 43. London: Home Office.

Maxfield, M. (1987b). Household Composition, routing activity and victimisation: a comparative analysis. *Journal of Quantitative Criminology,* 3, 301-320.

Maxfield, P. (1984). 'Target hardening—how much of an answer'. In Clarke, R. and Hope, T. (Eds.) *Coping with Burglary.* Boston, MA.: Kluwer-Nijhoff.

Mayhew, P. (1979). 'Defensible space: the current status of a crime prevention theory'. *Howard Journal,* XVIII, 150–159.

Merry, S. E. (1981). *Urban Danger: life in a neighbourhood of strangers.* Philadelphia: Temple University Press.

Morgan, P. (1978). *Delinquent Families.* London: Temple Smith.

Murray, C. (1990). *The Emerging Btitish Underclass.* London: The IEA Health and Welfare Unit.

Newman, O. (1973). *Defensible Space.* London: Architectural Press.

Osborn, S. and Bright, J. (1988). *Policing Housing Estates.* London: NACRO.

Parker, T. (1983). *The People of Providence.* London: Hutchinson.

Power, A. (1988). 'Housing, community and crime'. In Downes, D. *Crime and the City: essays in memory of John Barron Mays.* Basingstoke: Macmillan.

Power, A. (1984). *Local Housing Management.* London: Department of the Environment.

Power, A. (1987a). *Property Before People.* London: Allen and Unwin.

Power, A. (1987b). *The PEP Guide to Local Management.* Volume 1: The PEP Model. Volume 2: The PEP Experience. Volume 3: Guidelines for Setting Up New Projects. London: Department of the Environment.

Reiss, A. J. (1986). 'Why are communities important in understanding crime?'. In Reiss, A. J. and Tonry, M. (Eds.). *Communities and Crime. Crime and Justice: a review of research,* Vol. 8. Chicago: University of Chicago Press.

Reynolds, F. (1986). *The Problem Estate.* Aldershot: Gower.

Riley, D. and Shaw, M. (1985). *Parental Supervision and Juvenile Delinquency.* Home Office Research Study No. 83. London: HMSO.

Rock, P. (1988). 'Crime reduction initiatives on problem estates'. In Hope, T. and Shaw, M. (Eds.). *Communities and Crime Reduction.* London: HMSO.

Rosenbaum, D. P. (1988a). 'Community crime prevention: a review and synthesis of the literature'. *Justice Quarterly,* 5, pp. 323-395.

Rosenbaum, D. P. (1988b). 'A critical eye on neighbourhood watch: does it reduce crime and fear?' In Hope, T. and Shaw, M. (Eds.). *Communities and Crime Reduction.* London: HMSO.

Safe Neighbourhoods Unit (1985). *After Entryphones—improving management and security in multi-storey blocks.* London: Safe Neighbourhoods Unit.

Sampson, A. (1991). *Lessons from a Victim Support Crime Prevention Project.* Crime Prevention Unit Paper No. 25. London: Home Office.

Sampson, A. and Farrell, G. (1990). *Victim Support and Crime Prevention in an Inner-City Setting.* Crime Prevention Unit Paper No. 21. London: Home Office.

Shapland, J. and Vagg, J. (1988). *Policing by the Public.* London: Routledge.

Shaw, C. R. and McKay, H. D. (1969). *'Juvenile Delinquency and Urban Areas.* Chicago: University of Chicago Press.

Skogan, W. G. (1990). *Disorder and Decline.* New York: The Free Press.

Skogan, W. G. (1988a). 'Disorder, crime and community decline'. In Hope, T. and Shaw, M. (Eds.). *Communities and Crime Reduction.* London: HMSO.

Skogan, W. G. (1988b). 'Community organsiations and crime'. In Tonry, M. and Morris, N. (Eds.). *Crime and Justice: a review of research,* Vol. 10. Chicago: University of Chicago Press.

Skogan, W. G. and Maxfield, M. G. (1981). *Coping With Crime: individual and neighbourhood reactions.* Newbury Park, CA.: Sage Publications.

Skogan, W. G., Lewis, D. A., Podolefsky, A., DuBow, F., Gordon, M. T. (1982). *The Reactions to Crime Project*: executive summary. Washington, D.C.: U.S. Department of Justice.

Smith, D. J. (Ed.) (1992). *Understanding the Underclass.* London: Policy Studies Institute.

Sullivan, M. L. (1989). *'Getting Paid': youth crime and work in the inner city.* Ithaca, NY: Cornell University Press.

Suttles, G. D. (1972). *The Social Construction of Communities.* Chicago: University of Chicago Press.

Taub, R. P., Taylor, D. G. and Dunham, J. D. (1984). *Paths of Neighbourhood Change.* Chicago: University of Chicago Press.

Taylor, R. B. and Gottfredson, S. D. (1986). Environmental design, crime and prevention: an examination of community dynamics'. In Reiss, A. J. and Tonry, M. (Eds.). Communities and Crime. Crime and Justice: a review of research, Vol. 8. Chicago: University of Chicago Press.

Taylor, R. B., Gottfredson, S. D. and Brower, S. (1980). 'The defensibility of defensible space: a critical review and synthetic framework for future research. In Hirshi, T. and Gottfredson, M. (Eds.). *Understanding Crime.* Beverly Hills: Sage Publications.

Taylor, R. B. and Hale, M. (1986). 'Testing alternative models of fear of crime'. *Journal of Criminal Law and Criminology,* 77, pp. 151-189.

Willmott, P. and Murie, A. (1988). *Polarisation and Social Housing.* London: Policy Studies Institute.

Wilson, H. (1982). 'Delinquency and public housing: initiatives for future research'. In Hough, M. and Mayhew, P. (Eds.). *Crime and Public Housing.* Research and Planning Unit Paper 6. London: Home Office.

Wilson, H. (1980). 'Parental supervision and delinquency'. *British Journal of Criminology,* 20, pp. 203-35.

Wilson, J. Q. (1975). *Thinking About Crime.* New York: Basic Books.

Wilson, J. Q. and Kelling, G. (1982). 'Broken Windows'. *The Atlantic Monthly,* March, pp. 29-38.

Wilson, R. (1963). *Difficult Housing Estates.* Tavistock Pamphlet No. 5. London: Tavistock Publications.

Wilson, S. (1978). 'Vandalism and 'defensible space' on London housing estates'. In Clarke, R. V. G. (Ed.) *Tackling Vandalism.* Home Office Research Study No. 47. London: HMSO.

Wilson, W. J. (1987). *The Truly Disadvantaged Chicago:* University of Chicago Press.

Xanthos, P. (1989). In Bottoms, A. E., Mawby, R. I. and Xanthos, P. (1989). 'A tale of two estates'. In Downes, D. *Crime and the City: essays in memory of John Barron Mays.* Baingstoke: Macmillan.

Vancey, L. and Erikson, E. (1979). 'The antecedents of community: the economic and institutional structure of urban neighbourhoods'. *American Sociological Review,* 44, 253-62.

Publications

5. *Financial penalties and probation. Martin Davies. 1970. vii + 39pp.   (11 340105 1).
6. *Hostels for probationers. A study of the aims, working and variations in effectiveness of male probation hostels with special reference to the influence of the environment on delinquency. Ian Sinclair. 1971. ix + 200pp.   (11 340106 X).
7. *Prediction methods in criminology—including a prediction study of young men on probation. Frances H. Simon. 1971. xi + 234pp.   (11 340107 8).
8. *Study of the juvenile liaison scheme in West Ham 1961–65. Marilyn Taylor. 1971. vi + 46pp.   (11 340108 6).
9. *Explorations in after-care. I—After-care units in London, Liverpool and Manchester. Martin Silberman (Royal London Prisoners' Aid Society) and Brenda Chapman. II—After-care hostels receiving a Home Office grant. Ian Sinclair and David Snow (HORU). III—St. Martin of Tours House, Aryeh Leissner (National Bureau for Co-operation in Child Care). 1971. xi + 140pp.   (11 340109 4).
10. *A survey of adoption in Great Britain. Eleanor Grey in collaboration with Ronald M. Blunden. 1971. ix + 168pp.   (11 340110 8).
11. *Thirteen-year-old approved school boys in 1962s. Elizabeth Field, W. H. Hammond and J. Tizard. 1971. ix + 46pp.   (11 340111 6).
12. *Absconding from approved schools, R. V. G. Clarke and D. N. Martin. 1971. vi + 146pp.   (11 340112 4).
13. *An experiement in personality assessment of young men remanded in custody. H. Sylvia Anthony. 1972. viii + 79pp.   (11 340113 2).
14. *Girl offenders aged 17–20 years. I—Statistics relating to girl offenders aged 17–20 years from 1960 to 1970. II—Re-offending by girls released from borstal or detention centre training. III—The problems of girls released from borstal training during their period on after-care. Jean Davies and Nancy Goodman. 1972. v + 77pp.   (11 340114 0).
15. *The controlled trial in institutional research—paradigm or pitfall for penal evaluators? R. V. G. Clarke and D. B. Cornish. 1972. v + 33pp.   (11 340115 9).
16. *A survey of fine enforcement. Paul Softley. 1973. v + 65pp.   (11 340116 7).
17. *An index of social environment—designed for use in social work menum research. Martin Davies. 1973. vi + 63pp: (11 340117 5).
18. *Social enquiry reports and the probation service. Martin Davies and Andrea Knopf. 1973. v + 49pp.   (11 340118 3).
19. *Depression, psychopathic personality and attempted suicide in a borstal sample. H. Sylvia Anthony. 1973. viii + 44pp.   (0 11 340119 1).
20. *The use of bail and custody by London magistrates' courts before and after the Criminal Justice Act 1967, Frances Simon and Mollie Weatheritt. 1974. vi + 78pp.   (11 340120 5).
21. *Social work in the environment. A study of one aspect of probation practice. Martin Davies, with Margaret Rayfield, Alaster Calder and Tony Fowles. 1974. ix + 151pp.   (0 11 340102 7).
22. *Social work in prison. An experiment in the use of extended contact with offenders. Margaret Shaw. 1974. viii + 154pp.   (0 11 340122 1).
23. *Delinquency amongst opiate users. Joy Mott and Marilyn Taylor. 1974. vi + 31pp.   (0 11 340663 0).
24. *IMPACT. Intensive matched probation and after-care treatment. Vol. I—The design of the probation experiment and an interim evaluation. M. S. Folkard, A. J. Fowles, B. C. McWilliams, W. McWilliams, D. D. Smith, D. E. Smith and G. R. Walmsley. 1974. v + 54pp.   (0 11 340664 9).
25. *The approved school experience. An account of boys' experiences of training under differing regimes of approved schools, with an attempt to evaluate the effectiveness of that training. Anne B. Dunlop. 1974. vii + 124pp.   (0 11 340665 7).
26. *Absconding from open prisons. Charlotte Banks, Patricia Mayhew and R. J. Sapsford. 1975. viii + 89pp.   (0 11 340666 5).
27. *Driving while disqualified. Sue Kriefman. 1975. vi + 136pp.   (0 11 340667 3).

28. *Some male offenders' problems. I—Homeless offenders in Liverpool. W. McWilliams. II—Casework with short-term prisoners. Julie Holborn. 1975. x + 147pp. (0 11 340668 1).
29. *Community service orders. K. Pease, P. Durkin, I. Earnshaw, D. Payne and J. Thorpe. 1975. viii + 80pp. (0 11 340669 X).
30. *Field Wing Bail Hostel: the first nine months. Frances Simon and Sheena Wilson. 1975. viii + 55pp. (0 11 340670 3).
31. *Homicide in England and Wales 1967–1971. Evelyn Gibson. 1975. iv + 59pp. (0 11 340753 X).
32. *Residential treatment and its effects on delinquency. D. B. Cornish and R. V. G. Clarke. 1975. vi + 74pp. (0 11 340672 X).
33. *Further studies of female offenders. Part A: Borstal girls eight years after release. Nancy Goodman, Elizabeth Maloney and Jean Davies. Part B: The sentencing of women at the London Higher Courts. Nancy Goodman, Paul Durkin and Janet Halton. Part C: Girls appearing before a juvenile court. Jean Davies. 1976. vi + 114pp. (0 11 340673 8).
34. *Crime as opportunity. P. Mayhew, R. V. G. Clarke, A. Sturman and J. M. Hough. 1976. vii + 360pp. (0 11 340674 6).
35. *The effectiveness of sentencing: a rview of the literature. S. R. Brody. 1976. v + 89pp. (0 11 340675 4).
36. *IMPACT. Intensive matched probation and after-care treatment. Vol. II—The results of the experiment. M. S. Folkard, D. E. Smith and D. D. 1976. xi + 40pp. (0 11 340676 2).
37. *Police cautioning in England and Wales. J. A. Ditchfield. 1976. v + 31pp. (0 11 340677 0).
38. *Parole in England and Wales. C. P. Nuttall, with E. E. Barnard, A. J. Fowles, A. Frost, W. H. Hammond, P. Mayhew, K. Pease, R. Tarling and M. J. Weatheritt. 1977. vi + 90pp. (0 11 340678 9).
39. *Community service assessed in 1976. K. Pease, S. Bilingham and I. Earnshaw. 1977. vi + 29pp. (0 11 340679 7).
40. *Screen violence and film censorship: a review of research. Stephen Brody. 1977. vii + 179pp. (0 11 340680 0).
41. *Absconding from borstals. Gloria K. Laycock. 1977. v + 82pp. (0 11 340681 9).
42. *Gambling: a review of the literature and its implications for policy and research. D. B. Cornish. 1978. xii + 284pp. (0 11 340682 7).
43. *Compensation orders in magistrates' courts. Paul Softley. 1978. v + 41pp. (0 11 340683 5).
44. *Research in criminal justice. John Croft. 1978. iv + 16pp. (0 11 340684 3).
45. *Prison welfare: an account of an experiment at Liverpool. A. J. Fowles. 1978. v + 34pp. (0 11 340685 1).
46. *Fines in magistrates' courts. Paul Softley. 1978. v + 42pp. (0 11 340686 X).
47. *Tackling vandalism. R. V. Clarke (editor), F. J. Gladstone, A. Sturman and Sheena Wilson (contributors). 1978. vi + 91pp. (0 11 340687 8).
48. *Social inquiry reports: a survey. Jennifer Thorpe. 1979. vi + 55pp. (0 11 340688 6).
49. *Crime in public view. P. Mayhew, R. V. G. Clarke, J. N. Burrows, J. M. Hough and S. W. C. Winchester. 1979. v. + 36pp. (0 11 340689 4).
50. *Crime and the community. John Croft. 1979. v + 16pp. (0 11 340690 8).
51. *Life-sentence prisoners. David Smith (editor), Christopher Brown, Joan Worth, Roger Sapsford and Charlotte Banks (contributors). 1979. iv + 51pp. (0 11 340691 6).
52. *Hostels for offenders. Jane E. Andrews, with an appendix by Bill Sheppard. 1979. v + 30pp. (0 11 340692 4).
53. *Previous convictions, sentence and reconviction: a statistical study of a sample of 5,000 offenders convicted in January 1971. G. J. O. Phillpotts and L. B. Lancucki. 1979. v + 55pp. (0 11 340693 2).
54. *Sexual offences, consent and sentencing. Roy Walmsley and Karen White. 1979. vi + 77pp. (0 11 340694 0).
55. *Crime prevention and the police. John Burrows, Paul Ekblom and Keven Heal. 1979. v + 37pp. (0 11 340695 9).

56. *Sentencing practice in magistrates' courts. Roger Tarling, with the assistance of Mollie Weatheritt. 1979. vii + 54pp. (0 11 340696 7).
57. *Crime and comparative research. John Croft. 1979. iv + 16pp. (0 11 340697 5).
58. *Race, crime and arrests. Philip Stevens and Carole F. Willis. 1979. v + 69pp. (0 11 340698 3).
59. *Research and criminal policy. John Croft. 1980. iv + 14pp. (0 11 340699 1).
60. *Junior attendance centres. Anne B. Dunlop. 1980. v + 47pp. (0 11 340700 9).
61. *Police interrogation: an observational study in four police stations. Paul Softley, with the assistance of David Brown, Bob Forde, George Mair and David Moxon. 1980. vii+67pp. (0 11 340701 7).
62. *Co-ordinating crime prevention efforts. F. J. Gladstone. 1980. v+74pp. (0 11 340702 5).
63. *Crime prevention publicity: an assessment. D. Riley and P. Mayhew.1980. v+47pp. (0 11 340703 3).
64. *Taking offenders out of circulation. Stephen Brody and Roger Tarling. 1980. v+46pp. (0 11 340704 1).
65. *Alcoholism and social policy: are we on the right lines? Mary Tuck. 1980. v+30pp. (0 11 340701 7).
66. *Persistent petty offenders. Suzan Fairhead. 1981. vi+78pp. (0 11 340706 8).
67. *Crime control and the police. Pauline Morris and Kevin Heal. 1981. v+71pp. (0 11 340707 6).
68. *Ethnic minorities in Britain: a study of trends in their position since 1961. Simon Field, George Mair, Tom Rees and Philip Stevens. 1981. v+48pp. (0 11 340708 4).
69. *Managing criminological research. John Croft. 1981. iv+17pp. (0 11 340709 2).
70. *Ethnic minorities, crime and policing: a survey of the experiences of West Indians and whites. Mary Tuck and Peter Southgate. 1981. iv+54pp. (0 11 340765 3).
71. *Contested trials in magistrates' courts. Julie Vennard. 1982. v+32pp. (0 11 340766 1).
72. *Public disorder: a review of research and a study in one inner city area. Simon field and Peter Southgate. 1982. v+77pp. (0 11 340767 X).
73. *Clearing up crime. John Burrows and Roger Tarling. 1982. vii+31pp. (0 11 340768 8).
74. *Residential burglary: the limits of prevention. Stuart Winchester and Hilary Jackson. 1982. v+47pp. (0 11 340769 6).
75. *Concerning crime. John Croft. 1982. iv+16pp. (0 11 340770 X).
76. *The British Crime Survey: first report. Mike Hough and Pat Mayhew. 1983. v+62pp. (0 11 340786 6).
77. *Contacts between police and public: findings from the British Crime Survey. Peter Southgate and Paul Ekblom. 1984. v 42pp. (0 11 340771 8).
78. *Fear of crime in England and Wales. Michael Maxfield. 1984. v+57pp. (0 11 340772 6).
79. *Crime and police effectiveness. Ronald V Clarke and Mike Hough 1984. iv+33pp. (0 11 340773 3).
80. *The attitudes of ethnic minorities. Simon Field. 1984. v+49pp. (0 11 340774 2).
81. Victims of crime: the dimensions of risk. Michael Gottfredson. 1984. v + 54pp. (0 11 340775 0).
82. The tape recording of police interviews with suspects: an interim report. Carole Willis. 1984. v + 45pp. (0 11 340776 9).
83. Parental supervision and juvenile delinquency. David Riley and Margaret Shaw. 1985. v + 90pp. (0 11 340799 8).
84. Adult prisons and prisoners in England and Wales 1970-1982: a review of the findings of social research. Joy Mott. 1985. vi + 73pp. (0 11 340801 3).
85. Taking account of crime: key findings from the 1984 British Crime Survey. Mike Hogh and Pat Mayhew. 1985. vi + 115pp. (0 11 341810 2).
86. Implementing crime prevention measures. Tim Hope. 1985. vi + 82pp. (0 11 340812 9).
87. Resettling refugees: the lessons of research. Simon Field. 1985. vi + 66pp. (0 11 340815 3).

88. Investigating burglary: the measurement of police performance. John Burrows. 1986. vi + 36pp. (0 11 340824 2).
89. Personal violence. Roy Walmsley. 1986. vi + 87pp. (0 11 340827 7).
90. Police-public encounters. Peter Southgate. 1986. vi + 150pp. (0 11 340834 X).
91. Grievance procedures in prisons. John Ditchfield and Claire Austin. 1986. vi + 87pp. (0 11 340839 0).
92. The effectiveness of the Forensic Science Service. Malcolm Ramsay. 1987. v + 100) (0 11 340842 0).
93. The police complaints procedure: a survey of complainant's views. David Brown. 1987. v + 98pp. (0 11 340853 6).
94. The validity of the reconviction prediction score. Denis Ward. 1987. vi + 46pp. (0 11 340882 X).
95. Economic aspects of the illicit drug market enforcement policies in the United Kingdom. Adam Wagstaff and Alan Maynard. 1988. vii + 156pp. (0 11 340883 8).
96. Schools, disruptive behaviour and delinquency: a review of literature. John Graham. 1988. v + 70pp. (0 11 340887 0).
97. The tape recording of police interviews with suspects: a second interim report. Carole Willis, John Macleod and Peter Naish. 1988. vii + 97pp. (0 11 340890 0).
98. Triable-either-way cases: Crown Court or magistrate's court. David Riley and Julie Vennard. 1988. v + 52pp. (0 11 340891 9).
99. Directing patrol work: a study of uniformed policing. John Burrows and Helen Lewis. 1988 v + 66pp. (0 11 340891 9).
100. Probation day centres. George Mair. 1988. v + 44pp. (0 11 340894 3).
101. Amusement machines: dependency and delinquency. John Graham. 1988. v + 48pp. (0 11 340895 1).
102. The use and enforcement of compensation orders in magistrates' courts. Tim Newburn. 1988. v + 49pp. (0 11 340896 X).
103. Sentencing practice in the Crown Court. David Moxon. 1988. v + 90pp. (0 11 340902 8).
104. Detention at the police station under the Police and Criminal Evidence Act 1984. David Brown. 1988. v + 88pp. (0 11 340908 7).
105. Changes in rape offences and sentencing. Charles Lloyd and Ray Walmsley. 1989. vi + 53pp. (0 11 340910 9).
106. Concerns about rape. Lorna Smith. 1989. v + 48pp. (0 11 340911 7).
107. Domestic violence. Lorna Smith. 1989. v + 132pp. (0 11 340925 7).
108. Drinking and disorder: a study of non-metropolitan violence. Mary Tuck. 1989. v 111pp. (0 11 340926 5).
109. Special security units. Roy Walmsley. 1989. v + 114pp. (0 11 340961 3).
110. Pre-trial delay: the implications of time limits. Patricia Morgan and Julie Vennard. 1989. v + 66pp. (0 11 340964 8).
111. The 1988 British Crime Survey. Pat Mayhew, David Elliott and Lizanne Dowds. 1989. v + 133pp. (0 11 340965 6).
112. The settlement of claims at the Criminal Injuries Compensation Board. Tim Newburn. 1989. v + 40pp. (0 11 340967 2).
113. Race, community groups and service delivery. Hilary Jackson and Simon Field. 1989. v + 62pp. (0 11 340972 9).
114. Money payment supervision orders: probation policy and practice. George Mair and Charles Lloyd. 1989. v + 40pp. (0 11 340971 0).
115. Suicide and self-injury in prison: a literature review. Charles Lloyd. 1990. v + 69pp. (0 11 3409745 5).
116. Keeping in Touch: police-victim communication in two areas. Tim Newburn and Susan Merry. 1990. v + 52pp. (0 11 340974 5).
117. The police and public in England and Wales: a British Crime Survey report. Wesley G. Skogan. 1990. vi + 74pp. (0 11 340995 8).
118. Control in prisons: a review of the literature. John Ditchfield. 1990. (0 11 340996 6).

119. Trends in crime and their interpretation: a study of recorded crime in post-war England and Wales. Sinmon Field. 1990. (0 11 340994 X).
120. Electronic monitoring: the trials and their results. George Mair and Claire Nee. 1990. v + 79pp. (0 11 340998 2).
121. Drink driving: the effects of enforcement. David Riley. 1991. viii + 78pp. (0 11 340990 0).
122. Managing difficult prisoners: the Parkhurst Soecial Unit. Roy Walmsley (Ed.) 1991. x + 139pp. (0 11 341008 5).
123. Investigating burglary: the effects of PACE. David Brown. 1991. xii + 106pp. (0 11 341011 5).
124. Traffic policing in changing times. Peter Southgate and Catriona Mirlees-Black. 1991. viii + 139pp. (0 11 341019 0).
125. Magistrates' court or Crown Court? mode of trial decisions and sentencing. Carol Hedderman and David Moxon. 1992. vii + 53pp. (0 11 341036 0).
126. Developments in the use of compensation orders in magistrates' courts since October 1988. David Moxon, John Martin Corkery and Carol Hedderman. 1992. x + 48pp. (0 11 341042 5).
127. A comparative study of firefighting arrangements in Britain, Denmark, The Netherlands and Sweden. John Graham. Simon Field, Roger Tarling and Heather Wilkinson. 1992. x + 57pp. (0 11 341043 3).
128. The National Prison Survey 1991: main findings. Roy Walmsley, Liz Howard and Sheila White. 1992. xiv + 82pp. (0 11 341051 4).
129. Changing the Code: police detention under the revised PACE Codes of Practice. David Brown, Tom Ellis and Karen Larcombe. 1992. viii + 122pp. (0 11 341052 2).
130. Car theft: the offender's perspective. Roy Light, Claire Nee and Helen Ingham. 1993. x + 89pp. (0 11 341069 7).

ALSO

Designing out crime. R. V. G. Clarke and P. Mayhew (editors). 1980. viii+186pp. (0 11 340732 7).
(This book collects, with an introduction, studies that were originally published in HORS 34, 47, 49, 55, 62 and 63 and which are illustrative of the 'situational' approach to crime prevention.)

Policing today. Kevin Heal, Roger Tarling and John Burrows (editors). v+181pp. (0 11 340800 5).
(This book brings together twelve separate studies on police matters produced during the last few years by the Unit. The collection records some relatively little known contributions to the debate on policing.)

Managing Criminal Justice: a collection of papers. David Moxon (ed.). 1985. vi+222pp. (0 11 340811 0).
(This book brings together a number of studies bearing on the management of the criminal justice system. It includes papers by social scientists and operational researchers working within the Research and Planning Unit, and academic researchers who have studied particular aspects of the criminal process.)

Situational Crime Prevention: from theory into practice. Kevin Heal and Gloria Laycock (editors).
1986. vii+166pp. (0 11 340826 9).
(Following the publication of *Designing Out Crime,* further research has been completed on the theoretical background to crime prevention. In drawing this work together this book sets down some of the theoretical concerns and discusses the emerging practical issues. It includes contributions by Unit staff as well as academics from this country and abroad.)

115

Communities and crime reduction. Tim Hope and Margaret Shaw (eds.). 1988. vii+311pp. (11 340892 7).
(The central theme of this book is the possibility of preventing crime by building upon the resources of local communities and of active citizens. The specially commissioned chapters, by distinguished international authors, review contemporary research and policy on community crime prevention.)

New directions in police training. Peter Southgate (ed.). 1988. xi+256pp. (11 340889 7).
(Training is central to the development of the police role, and particular thought and effort now go into making it more responsive current needs—in order to produce police officers who are both effective and sensitive in their dealing with the public. This book illustrates some of the thinking and research behind these developments.)

The above HMSO publications can be purchased from Government Bookshops or through booksellers.

The following Home Office research publications are available on request from the Home Office Research and Planning Unit, 50 Queen Anne's Gate, London SW1H 9AT.

Research Unit Papers (RUP)

1. Uniformed police work and management technology. J. M. Hough. 1980.
2. Supplementary information on sexual offences and sentencing. Roy Walmsley and Karen White. 1980.
3. Board of visitor adjudications. David Smith, Claire Austin and John Ditchfield. 1981.
4. Day centres and probation. Suzan Fairhead, with the assistance of J. Wilkinson-Grey. 1981.

Research and Planning Unit Papers (RPUP)

5. Ethnic minorities and complaints against the police. Philip Stevens and Carole Willis. 1982.
6. *Crime and public housing. Mike Hough and Pat Mayhew (editors). 1982.
7. Abstracts of race relations research. George Mair and Philip Stevens (editors). 1982.
8. Police probationer training in race relations. Peter Southgate. 1982.
9. *The police response to calls from the public. Paul Ekblom and Kevin Heal. 1982.
10. City centre crime: a situational approach to prevention. Malcolm Ramsay. 1982.
11. Burglary in schools: the prospects for prevention. Tim Hope. 1982.
12. *Fine enforcement. Paul Softley and David Moxon. 1982.
13. Vietnamese refugees. Peter Jones. 1982.
14. Community resources for victims of crime. Karen Williams. 1983.
15. The use, effectiveness and impact of police stop and search powers. Carole Willis. 1983.
16. Acquittal rates. Sid Butler. 1983.
17. Criminal justice comparisons: the case of Scotland and England and Wales. Loma J. F. Smith. 1983.

18. Time taken to deal with juveniles under criminal proceedings. Catherine Frankenburg and Roger Tarling. 1983.

19. Civilian review of complaints against the police: a survey of the United States literature. David C. Brown. 1983.

20. Police action on motoring offences. David Riley. 1983.

21. *Diverting drunks from the criminal justice system. Sue Kingsley and George Mair. 1983.

22. The staff resource implications of an independent prosecution system. Peter R. Jones. 1983.

23. Reducing the prison population: an exploratory study in Hampshire. David Smith, Bill Sheppard, George Mair, Karen Williams, 1984.

24. Criminal justice system model: magistrates' courts sub-model. Susan Rice. 1984.

25. Measures of police effectiveness and efficiency. Ian Sinclair and Clive Miller. 1984.

26. Punishment practice by prison Boards of Visitors. Susan Iles, Adrienne Connors, Chris May, Joy Mott. 1984.

27. *Reparation, conciliation and mediation: current projects and plans in England and Wales. Tony Marshall. 1984.

28. Magistrates' domestic courts: new perspectives. Tony Marshall (editor). 1984.

29. Racism awareness training for the police. Peter Southgate. 1984.

30. Community constables: a study of a policing initiative. David Brown and Susan Iles. 1985.

31. Recruiting volunteers. Hilary Jackson. 1985.

32. Juvenile sentencing: is there a tariff? David Moxon, Peter Jones, Roger Tarling. 1985.

33. Bringing people together: mediation and reparation projects in Great Britain. Tony Marshall and Martin Walpole. 1985.

34. Remands in the absence of the accused. Chris May. 1985.

35. Modelling the criminal justice system. Patricia M. Morgan. 1985.

36. The criminal justice system model: the flow model. Hugh Pullinger. 1986.

37. Burglary: police actions and victim views. John Burrows. 1986.

38. Unlocking community resources: four experimental government small grants schemes. Hilary Jackson. 1986.

39. The cost of discriminating: a review of the literature. Shirley Dex. 1986.

40. Waiting for Crown Court trial: the remand population. Rachel Pearce. 1987.

41. Children's evidence the need for corroboration. Carol Hedderman. 1987.

42. A preliminary study of victim offender mediation and reparation schemes in England & Wales. Gwynn Davis, Jacky Boucherat, David Watson, Adrian Thatcher (Consultant). 1987.

43. Explaining fear of crime: evidence from the 1984 British Crime Survey. Michael Maxfield. 1987.

44. Judgements of crime seriousness: evidence from the 1984 British Crime Survey. Ken Pease. 1988.

45. Waiting time on the day in magistrates' courts: a review of case listings practises. David Moxon and Roger Tarling (editors). 1988.

46. Bail and probation work: the ILPS temporary bail action project. George Mair, 1988.
47. Police work and manpower allocation. Roger Tarling. 1988.
48. Computers in the courtroom. Carol Hedderman. 1988.
49. Data interchange between magistrates' courts and other agencies. Carol Hedderman. 1988.
50. Bail and probation work II: the use of London probation/bail hostels for bailees. Helen Lewis and George Mair. 1989.
51. The role and function of police community liaison officers. Susan V. Phillips and Raymond Cochrane. 1989.
52. Insuring against burglary losses. Helen Lewis. 1989.
53. Remand decisions in Brighton and Bournemouth. Patricia Morgan and Rachel Pearce. 1989.
54. Racially motivated incidents reported to the police. Jayne Seagrave. 1989.
55. Review of research on re-offending of mentally disordered offenders. David J. Murray. 1990.
56. Risk prediction and probation: papers from a Research and Planning Unit workshop. George Mair (editor). 1990.
57. Household fires: findings from the British Crime Survey 1988. Chris May. 1990.
58. Home Office funding of victim support schemes—money well spent?. Justin Russell. 1990.
59. Unit fines: experiments in four courts. David Moxon, Mike Sutton and Carol Hedderman. 1990.
60. Deductions from benefit for fine default. David Moxon, Carol Hedderman and Mike Sutton. 1990.
61. Monitoring time limits on custodial remands. Paul F. Henderson. 1991.
62. Remands in custody for up to 28 days: the experiments. Paul F. Henderson and Patricia Morgan. 1991.
63. Parenthood training for young offenders: an evaluation of courses in Young Offenders Institutions. Diane Caddle. 1991.
64. The multi-agency approach in practice: the North Plaistow racial harassment project. William Saulsbury and Benjamin Bowling. 1991.
65. Offending while on bail: a survey of recent studies. Patricia M. Morgan. 1992.
66. Juveniles sentenced for serious offences: a comparison of regimes in Young Offender Institutions and Local Authority Community Homes. John Ditchfield and Liza Catan. 1992.
67. The management and deployment of police armed response vehicles. Peter Southgate. 1992.
68. Using psychometric personality tests in the selection of firearms officers. Catriona Mirrlees-Black. 1992.
69. Bail information schemes: practice and effect. Charles Lloyd. 1992.
70. Crack and cocaine in England and Wales. Joy Mott (editor). 1992.
72. The National Probation Survey 1990. Chris May. 1993.
73. Public satisfaction with police services. Peter Southgate and Debbie Crisp. 1993.
74. Disqualification from driving: an effective penalty? Catriona Mirrlees-Black. 1993.
75. Detention under the Prevention of Terrorism (Temporary Provisions) Act 1989: Access to legal advice and outside contact. David Brown. 1993.

Research Bulletin
The Research Bulletin is published twice a year and consists mainly of short articles relating to projects which are part of the Home Office Research and Planning Unit's research programme.

Printed in the United Kingdom for HMSO
Dd296226 6/93 C10 G3397 10170